"PUBLIC SECRETS" AS A PHENOMENON IN ORGANIZATIONAL COMMUNICATION: HOW PUBLIC KNOWLEDGE FAILS TO BECOME ORGANIZATIONAL ACTION

"Public Secrets" as a Phenomenon in Organizational Communication: How Public Knowledge Fails to Become Organizational Action

Xin-An Lu

iUniverse, Inc.

New York Lincoln Shanghai

"Public Secrets" as a Phenomenon in Organizational
Communication: How Public Knowledge Fails to Become
Organizational Action

iUniverse, Inc.

For information address:
iUniverse, Inc.
2021 Pine Lake Road, Suite 100
Lincoln, NE 68512
www.iuniverse.com

ISBN: 0-595-27370-X

Printed in the United States of America

CONTENTS

LIST OF ILLUSTRATIONS

LIST OF TABLES

ABSTRACT

Drawing on literature addressing systems theory, dichotomies in the organization, the cultural phenomenon of taboo, defensive communication and information distortion, the learning organization, and employee motivation, this study examines an under-researched phenomenon in organizational communication that the author labels as "public secrets." This is a phenomenon in which people express their genuine feelings, understandings, and knowledge about their organization in one context (e.g., informally with family, friends, and colleagues), but not in another context (e.g., formally at public conferences or with administrators). The study will define the phenomenon of public secrets and explore the causes, consequences, and strategies for this phenomenon.

The subject organization for this study was a large public research institution in the Midwest. Five hundred faculty members were contacted through electronic mail. Three hundred and eight tenured and non-tenured faculty members responded to the Web-based survey of this study. Ten faculty members were also interviewed as a validation for the process and results of the survey.

Results from the study revealed that the communication phenomenon of public secrets does exist in the organizational setting, and that, in the case of the subject organization, this phenomenon exists among the majority of the organizational members. A survey instrument was designed to solicit respondents' perception of possible causes and consequences of public secrets, topics involved in public secrets, and strategies to alleviate the phenomenon of public secrets. The findings demonstrate that "lack of interaction opportunities with administration" and "suggestions ignored" are among the top causes of public secrets. "Bad communication climate" and "low morale" are among the top consequences from public secrets. Topics that are most often avoided in public/formal discussion are "colleague performance" and "administration practices." Most effective strategies to alleviate the phenomenon of public secrets include "acknowledging suggestions with action" and "discussion of 'undiscussables' initiated by administration." Regarding respondents' practice of public secrets, no significant differences were found between different groups in terms of sex, tenure, years of work experience, salary range, and academic unit.

ACKNOWLEDGEMENTS

My thanks first go to Dr. Mary Lou Higgerson. She teaches, helps, and influences me—both through her learning and her being. Her constant, prompt, and thoughtful guidance and care prove an indispensable asset for the satisfactory completion of my doctoral studies here at Southern Illinois University at Carbondale. My thanks for Dr. Higgerson will remain long after completion of this research project.

Second, my thanks go to the other members on the committee: Dr. Laurel Hetherington, Dr. Daradirek (Gee) Ekachai, Dr. Richard Lanigan, Dr. Nilanjana Bardhan, and Dr. Allan Karnes. Their insightful criticism and suggestions are a great contribution to a quality completion of this dissertation. I also wish to acknowledge their kind help that goes beyond my academic work.

Third, my thanks go to many of my colleagues, and J.P. Dunn and Roberta Reeves of the Instructional Support Service at Morris Library. This project received much help of various kinds from many of my colleagues. Mel Bower, for instance, willingly accepted the chore of proofreading the draft of the dissertation. Some colleagues' stimulating academic dialogue with me served as a great motivation of the progress of the project. Help from J.P. Dunn and Roberta Reeves saved me a great amount of time in designing the on-line survey form and in the electronic management of data entry.

Last, but surely not least, I would like to thank my dear family for reasons that are well-known to conventional understanding—everything that the husband does has a concomitant invisible contribution from the family.

1
INTRODUCTION

PREFACE

If what is said is not what is meant,
    what ought to be done remains undone;
If what ought to be done remains undone,
    morals and art are corrupted;
If morals and art are corrupted,
    justice will go astray,
    and the people will stand about in helpless confusion.

—a Chinese sage.

It was the beginning of April, 1999. The weather was becoming very hot. I was sitting in the Student Center eating my lunch. Despite the very hot weather, the heating was on in the Student Center. After disburdening myself of all unnecessary clothes, I still felt so hot that it bordered on pain to sit in the Student Center having my lunch. Everybody there felt hot, but nobody there could make any change. We did not know where to access the control to turn off the heating system. Somebody surely knew this, but we did not know who this person was. Thus it was known to everyone in the Student Center that the heating was making the temperature intolerably high, yet this was a secret or unknown information to the person possessing control access over the heating system. Consequently, people in the Student Center suffered helplessly—with clear and direct knowledge of the cause of their misery.

In many organizations, people possess knowledge about organizational problems and causes of these problems, yet they do not possess the power to act upon such knowledge. On the other hand, organizational management and leadership possess the power to act upon essential organizational information and knowledge, yet they frequently do not have this essential information and knowledge. This awkward and sometimes dysfunctional situation is rather like an information-possessing eye that is disconnected with the order-giving brain. Such a configuration may cause one tragedy where the eye sees the body walking over the cliff and yet can do nothing to prevent it.

In numerous organizations, managers and leaders maintain the power to effect major changes and then cut or hide themselves away from the public. The general organization members, deprived of the discretionary power to initiate actions, may helplessly and repeatedly suffer from the same mistakes, pain or even inhumanity, while clearly knowing the causes of such mistakes, pain or inhumanity. This problem of mismatched distributions of power and knowledge, to a great extent, comes from a negative organizational communication phenomenon that I call "public secrets."

It is a rather widespread phenomenon in organizational communication in which general organization members express their true feelings and understandings about their workplace in one context (especially informally with colleagues, friends, and family), but not in anther context (especially formally at public meetings or with their bosses). As a result, much knowledge and information that is public in one context is secret or unavailable in another context. In simpler words, such knowledge is a secret that many know, perhaps except for "the dominant coalition" or those in positions to make organizational decisions. Hence, the term of "public secrets" seems to be an appropriate label for this phenomenon. As expressed by a vice-president of a Fortune 500 company, the problem is "all the time people spend in meetings not saying what's really on their minds" (Ryan and Oestreich, 1991, p. xiii). Consequently, on one hand, management and leadership may complain that they are plagued with a myriad of organizational problems and yet possess inadequate information to make viable decisions. The task of management and leadership, many managers and leaders claim, is becoming more and more difficult.

On the other hand, general organization members remain rather nonchalant about their workplace when they find that their genuine knowledge about their workplace can only remain public informally with friends, colleagues, and family. When it comes to formal communication situations including conferences and conversations with bosses, they believe it safer to keep secret their genuine knowledge about their workplace. As a result, organization members may easily perceive that many organizational regulations, policies, plans, budgetary distribution, and orders are irrelevant in the sense that these things do not directly address what they believe should be addressed. Nothing is perhaps more demotivating and debilitating than engaging one's energy and time in things that one perceives as "irrelevant," in things that do not conform with one's beliefs, values, and knowledge.

The organizational phenomenon of public secrets not only leads to an organizational agenda that organization members may *perceive* as irrelevant, it may well lead to an organizational agenda that actually *is* irrelevant. Without adequate absorption and use of first-hand information from frontline organization members who are the closest to various aspects of the organizational reality, management and leadership may work with their own imaginations rather than the hard organizational reality. The resultant rift between general organization members on one hand, and the management and leadership on the other makes the matter worse. This rift can cripple communication and information flow within the organization. What all this cultivates is an organizational climate that is poor in trust but rich in offense and defense.

In a defensive communication climate, people may make more efforts to circle and cover up and justify problems rather than to directly endeavor to solve the problems. This job of circling and covering up and justifying problems and all its consequences consume vast amounts of human and material resources for no reason or for negative reasons. All this leads to what I call an agenda of mediocrity—an agenda of irrelevances, insignificances, busy work, complications, and confusions. The agenda of mediocrity, as a result of "public secrets," is extremely demotivating and wasteful. People's inability to transform their sharable knowledge into "actionable" knowledge[1] vibrates debilitating disillusionment throughout the organization. When public secrets *are* transformed into public knowledge, this new public knowledge would become powerful guidelines, and people would be liberated from the complicated and debilitating toil of mediocrity that involves unnecessary overlapped work, complications, and wasteful bureaucracies. With this liberation, people would be able to engage in the simple art of greatness, which is concerted effort directed headlong against what really needs to be done. With this liberation, people would be able to think what they live, and live what they think, and thus have personal and public integrity. With this liberation, leading a big company may be as straightforward as "cooking a small fish," as said by Confucius. That is, leading a big company is no longer the complicated struggle of manipulative power and politics, but becomes the simple and neat joy of facilitating the natural emergence and fulfillment of common dreams.

Public secrets as a possibly widespread organizational communication phenomenon is far from well studied. "Public secrets" even as a term seems absent in the literature of organizational communication. My search of available literature produced little concerning public secrets as an organizational communication phenomenon. Public secrets as a possibly common phenomenon in organizational communication that seems to exert great impact on organizational operation and health necessarily merit more academic attention.

---

1.   Distinction between sharable knowledge and "actionable" knowledge will be explained in the following section of Chapter One.

With a triangulated research methodology that involves case illustrations, interviews, and Web-based surveys, this study explores the following research questions:

RQ1:   Does the organizational communication phenomenon of public secrets exist, and, if yes, how widespread is this phenomenon?

RQ2:   What factors do respondents perceive as contributing to the emergence of public secrets?

RQ3:   What do respondents perceive as the impact of public secrets on organizational health and organizational members' quality of work?

RQ4:   In what areas do public secrets exist?

RQ5:   Are the suggested strategies to allay the phenomenon of public secrets effective in respondents' perception?

DEFINITIONS AND CHARACTERISTICS OF PUBLIC SECRETS

I define public secrets as organizational information/knowledge that is explicitly expressed and exchanged in one communication context (especially the informal/unofficial context) by part or all organization members but kept secret/tacit in another communication context (especially the formal/official context) to another group of organization members (usually the management and leadership).

I would like to explain what I mean by this conceptual definition. First, public secrets involve organizational information, not private information. For instance, Tom has three brothers. Tom shares this information with five of his co-workers. Other co-workers and Tom's managers do not know this information. This type of information, though shared or public within one group but secret to another group, does not belong to what I define as "public secrets," because this type of information is not organizational but private in nature. Private information is that which barely has anything to do with the organization's operation and health. And private information is usually constitutionally protected. It would be unadvisable to encourage study of such information in the discipline of organizational communication. Organizational information should have direct bearing upon the organization's operation and health. Such information may include management practices, the financial budget, personnel changes, compensation and benefits, the organizational goals and values, and the like.

Second, public secrets obviously represent an oxymoron. One side of this oxymoron is the public/known side of public secrets. In other words, public secrets contain clear, understood, and shared knowledge/information. This knowledge is similar to but not exactly the same as "explicit knowledge" defined by Nonaka and Takeuchi (1995).

According to Nonaka and Takeuchi (1995), there are two types of knowledge that helps an organization learn, tacit knowledge and explicit knowledge. Tacit knowledge is usually possessed by individual organization members. This type of knowledge is tacit because it is not easily visible and expressible. Tacit knowledge includes individuals' private beliefs, understandings, unexpressed information, subtle techniques accumulated through long experience, general feelings, and rough concepts. Explicit knowledge, on the other hand, can easily be expressed, processed, and transmitted, electronically or otherwise. Explicit knowledge is usually systematically recorded in organizational documents, regulations, agendas, pamphlets and the like, making this type of knowledge easily retrievable.

Nonaka and Takeuchi's (1995) "explicit knowledge" is not only easily expressible and shared by many, but also is usually incorporated in the process of the organization's policy formulation. This means that "explicit knowledge" is able to influence organizational actions. The public side of "public secrets," however, is clearly known, expressed, and shared only among a limited group of people in a limited context (usually the informal communication context). The explicit information contained in public secrets usually does not enter the process of policy formulation. That is why public secrets are still secrets to some group of organization members, more often the decision-makers of the organization. The number of people who know and share the information contained in public secrets may vary. Sometimes, it may only be a coterie of those well-informed members. More often, information in public secrets is known and shared among a large number of people or even among all the organization members, though in a restricted context.

The other side of the oxymoron of public secrets is the secret side. Information contained in a "public secret" must be unknown in some context and/or to some group of people, either in the literal sense or in the figurative sense. By "figuratively unknown," I mean that the information is actually known, but not officially recognized, communicated, or disseminated. For example, managers and leaders may clearly know that a rumor is circulating among a large number of organization members, but they may deliberately deny, in public/official situations, their knowledge of the rumor, thus shirking the obligation to incorporate "unpleasant" information into organizational policy formulation.

The secret side of public secrets is different from "tacit knowledge" as defined by Nonaka and Takeuchi (1995), which is knowledge latent within the individual in the form of feelings, intuitions, and personal techniques. Tacit knowledge is not amenable to easy expression. Information contained in "public secrets," however, is not latent in individual organization members. This information is expressible, expressed, and shared. It is only that this information is secret to or not formally recognized by some other section of organization members (usually the section at the top of the organizational pyramid).

The information contained in public secrets is usually known and shared in informal situations like social interactions among co-workers, family, and friends. Yet in some cases, public secrets may contain information known only to a small coterie of managers and leaders, but kept secret to general organization members. In this latter situation, public secrets may represent a deliberate or actual failure in downward organizational communication.

To enable a better understanding of the concept of "public secrets," I would like to talk about the distinction between sharable knowledge and actionable knowledge.

Sharable knowledge means knowledge/information that is expressible, expressed, transmitted, and shared. This knowledge exists in its native, passive form of mere knowledge, barely serving as guidance for or exerting impact upon organizational actions. Sharable knowledge exists without actual application, rather like the dead knowledge that students acquire from some old textbooks. This type of knowledge may be always there in the brain but never comes down to the hands in some tangible form of guidance for, application into, or transformation of reality.

Actionable knowledge, on the other hand, is knowledge to act upon, knowledge to direct actions, knowledge to effect changes, or, in short, knowledge for applications. Assumptions, values, logic, and information from organizational survey results, for example, that contribute to the formulation of organizational goals, policies, rules, regulations, are all actionable knowledge because they affect, direct, and produce organizational actions.

Information in public secrets usually exists in the form of sharable knowledge, but not in the form of actionable knowledge. This adds a tragic flavor to public secrets. That is, information/knowledge in public secrets is rather dead and useless in terms of its ability to improve an organization's operation and health. The Challenger disaster, which I will address later on in this chapter, is a good illustration.

The grapevine is a typical form of informal organizational communication channel along which public secrets travel. There is a popular conception, especially among management and leadership, that the grapevine only promotes false and nasty rumors and results in tainted names and hurt feelings. Because of all these negative associations with the grapevine, organizations have been trying to get rid of the grapevine for many years. Yet the interesting result is that the harder the organization tries to abolish the grapevine, the more prosperous it becomes (Davis, 1973). Restricting informal information flow only serves to increase organization members' ambiguities and need for more relevant information. The more they seek information, the more they seek to develop the informal communication lines like the grapevine. Public secrets, which can be manifested as rumors along the grapevine, may be a major form of information that flows along the informal organizational communication lines. Therefore, it may be claimed that public secrets are a by-product of the organization's attempt to restrict its informal organizational communication channels. The greater the degree of public secrets within an organization, the greater may be this organization's attempt to restrict its informal organizational communication channels, or vice versa.

The grapevine spreads information fast, perhaps faster than any organizational document can ever hope to achieve. Information along the grapevine goes in a fluid, unpredictable, and multidirectional manner, and multiplies itself in explosive and geometric progression. The transmitive or communicative power of the grapevine is amazing also because employees often find the grapevine more believable than management. As we all know, the word of mouth has wings (please refer to figure 1.1 for a visual illustration of the transmitive power of the grapevine).

Although the grapevine is an inevitable and powerful part of organizational communication, 92.4% of companies surveyed by Crampton, Hodge, and Mishra (1998) had no policy to deal with the grapevine, and managers and organizations usually did not take an active role in dealing with informal communication networks.

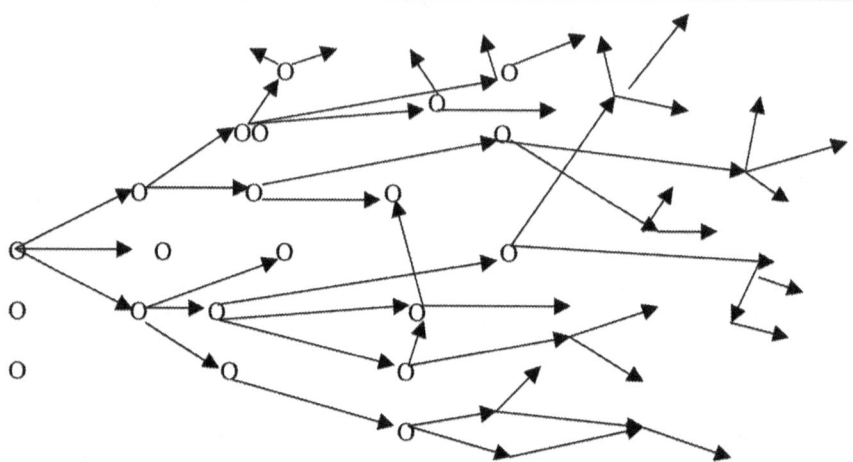

Figure 1.1 The Communicative Power of the Grapevine or the Word of Mouth

"Public secrets," because they generally flow along the grapevine, possess great velocity in dissemination. Consequently, this velocity may make the "public" side of "public secrets" much bigger, and the "secret" side of "public secrets" much smaller. Generally speaking, "public secrets" are like an inverted iceberg. The exposed part is big, and the hidden part is small, meaning that "public secrets" are usually public to a large number of people but secret to a small number of people or in a restricted communication context. This frequently grants great popularity and power to the information contained in public secrets, making public secrets a phenomenon that is not to be casually ignored. This also makes the organization's fight against public secrets through further information restriction a wasted effort, if not a fiasco.

Public secrets, because of the characteristics of informal communication channels, not only enjoy great dissemination speed, but also frequently possess more information accuracy and credibility than what comes down along the formal communication lines. According to Davis and O'Conner (1977), in informal communication, there are far more opportunities for feedback; there are fewer status discrepancies among informal communicators, making it less risky for feedback to be sought; and there are more opportunities for message redundancies in informal communication lines, allowing the organization members to hear the same information from several sources (reference may be made again to figure 1.1 on page 10). Because of all these features, informal communication does not suffer from problems like easy distortion in serial, formal communication. Information in public secrets generally contains great accuracy and credibility because it usually travels along the informal communication lines. Rumors, contrary to popular perception, are frequently accurate reflection of reality. Karathanos and Auriemmo (1999) believe that the grapevine or the informal communication network is an invaluable asset to an organization. Instead of pruning the grapevine, which is unwarranted and unproductive, managers and leaders should nurture it and try to incorporate it into their organization's formal communication system. By doing this, Karathanos and Auriemmo contend, the organization will reap great "grapes" or benefits.

Communication is a free-flowing liquid. It seeks and spreads itself through all possible crevices and chinks. It is extremely difficult to contain communication within one channel if the channel is too narrow and inadequate. The attempt to force all information or communication into one stipulated channel that more often than not proves narrow and inadequate may cause the information or communication to "burst" out into other channels, like what occurs with a flood. It may be claimed that public secrets are frequently communicational seepage out of the official communication pipeline. Public secrets are symptomatic of a leaking, inadequate, and dysfunctional organizational communication pipeline, often indicating a failure of the organization's upward communication line. Being unable to flow vertically upward along the official communication line, the information contained in public secrets often can only stay horizontally among general organization members in the free-flowing, grapevine fashion. This inability to get into the official communication line prevents information contained in public secrets from becoming the organization's actionable knowledge to guide organizational actions. Consequently, the rich river of untapped informational resources in public secrets meanders and wanders in a wasted form, irrigating nothing but the weeds of cynicism and alienation. Another analogy may be appropriate. If Drucker (1993) is correct by saying that information is *the* resource that the modern organization can hope to possess, then information can be compared to blood that provides for an organization's life. Too much information leakage in the form of public secrets may ultimately "bleed" an organization to death, both internally and externally.

According to Fisher (1981), "there is no such thing as 'lack of communication.'" (p. 11). "Lack of communication" only comes from impoverished interpretation through impoverished channels. Public secrets are the product from managers' and leaders' over-dependence upon inadequate formal and downward communication channels. Without giving enough attention to informal and upward communication channels, managers and leaders will inevitably be plagued with the make-believe problem of "lack of communication or information." No organization, according to Fisher, is plagued with a poverty of information; the organization can only be plagued with a poverty of effort to exploit its existing informational reserves. Public secrets may be symptomatic of the organization's poverty in effort to tap its existing informational reserves.

Operationally, I define public secrets as a communicational inconsistency that indicates or measures possible organizational disease. This communicational inconsistency can be acquired through a contrast between results from facilitated informal communication channels and documentation of official communication. Facilitated informal communication channels may include organizational ethnography, interviews, surveys, and other investigation/measurement instruments.

Documentation of official communication may include employee manuals, information sheets, newsletters, and house organs.

More specifically in terms of this study, I conducted surveys and interviews to acquire data about the phenomenon of public secrets within the workplace. Responses from these interviews and surveys were used to determine the existence and the degree of existence of public secrets within the organizational setting. To illustrate, a positive response to the question, "Do you express and exchange frank opinions about your institution with colleagues, friends, and/or family, but not with administrators?" indicates the existence of public secrets at the subject institution. An "always" choice (instead of the other response choices of "twice a day," "twice a week"…) in response to the question, "How often do you express frank opinions about your institution informally, but not formally?" indicates a strong degree of existence of public secrets in the respondents' institution. In short, for this study, public secrets is operationally defined through means of participants' responses to a multi-item index, ranging from "always" to "never," from "not important" to "very important," or from "not effective" to "very effective," depending on the type of questions the respondents were asked.

Public secrets, as I claimed, may be symptomatic of possible organizational disease. This disease is manifested, among other things, through an inconsistency between the organization's formal and informal communications. The greater this inconsistency, the more severe the organizational disease may be. The operational problem here lies with the measurement of this inconsistency. I would suggest public secrets as one measurement tool or barometer of possible organizational disease. The amount and degree of public secrets can be roughly acquired through facilitated informal communication channels where organization members are enabled to explicitly express their genuine ideas about their workplace, and where their expressions can be recorded. Then a contrast and comparison should be made between this facilitated record and the documentation of the organization's official communication (e.g., employee manuals, information sheets, newsletters, house organs). Since there is no official documentation of the organization members' informal communication, this documentation has to be created by and for research. The number of inconsistencies between the research-facilitated documentation and the organization's official documentation would help indicate the amount and degree of inconsistencies between the organization's informal and formal communications. The greater the degree and amount of these inconsistencies, the more severe the problem of public secrets, and in turn the more diseased the organization is in its communication. Of course further research is needed to test this hypothesis and to determine the exact relationship between public secrets and organizational health.

The communication structure in an organization is a system. A well-functioning system possesses interdependence, cooperation, and congruence among the various components of the system. Public secrets, as a reflection of the inconsistency or incompatibility between the formal and informal communications within an organization, indicate a dysfunctional communication system within the organization.

Organizational communication is highly multidimensional like all other forms of communication. For example, the multidimensionality of general communication can be explained through the easy dichotomy of verbal and nonverbal communication. Similarly, the multidimensionality of organizational communication can also be explained through the dichotomy of informal and official communication. When there is discrepancy between verbal and nonverbal communication, people choose to go with the latter. Similarly, when there is a discrepancy between the organization's official and informal communication, people usually choose to go with the informal communication.

According to Fisher (1981), nonverbal communication not only enjoys much credibility, but also may contain more information than verbal communication does. Consequently, nonverbal communication may affect more attitude change than verbal communication. By citing the experiment by Mehrabian and Ferris (1967), Fisher informs that only 7% of attitude change was accounted for by the verbal content of the message, while 38% of attitude change was accounted for by vocal characteristics, and 55% was accounted for by facial expressions.

Similarly, information contained in public secrets usually is more credible and more revealing than what comes down through the official or formal communication channels. As a result, information contained in public secrets frequently has more impact upon and is more indicative of organizational members' attitude, mood, morale, and motivation. If there is a dichotomy of formal and informal communications within the organization, there should also be a dichotomy between organizational members' compliant action and committed action, or between organization members' performance and being. We may also say that the formal organizational communication influences organizational members' compliance and performance, and the informal organizational communication influences organization members' commitment and being. Frequently, organizational members believe that what is not officially communicated about their organization says more than what is. Therefore, public secrets, a major type of communication that goes along the organization's unofficial communication lines, promise to have great impact upon organizational operation and health.

Assisted by conceptual and operational definitions of public secrets, the reader may see that public secrets can exist in a variety of settings and in a variety of forms. For example, secrets in the family may become expressed and shared information with strangers on a plane journey. Secrets in peaceful time may become shared knowledge in war or other disasters like an earthquake. The vice versa may also be true. What is considered taboo and secret in one culture may be daily practice in another culture. More specifically in the organizational setting, public secrets may exist in the following forms: (1) Public knowledge among general organization members is kept secret and tacit when it comes to managers and administrators; (2) Knowledge shared in informal settings (e.g., in the hallway, at off-work time and locations) is kept secret and tacit in formal settings (e.g., organizational meetings and documents); (3) Public knowledge among managers and administrators is kept secret and tacit for general organizational members; and (4) Public knowledge shared among one group of organizational members is kept secret and tacit to and/or among another group. The study for this project focuses more on public secrets that exist in the first two forms with an emphasis on the dichotomy between general organizational members and the informal organizational communication context on one hand, and managers, administrators, and the formal organizational communication context on the other hand.

For a more empirical understanding of the phenomenon of "public secrets," the following section offers cases that help provide a more concrete picture of public secrets.

ILLUSTRATIONS OF PUBLIC SECRETS

Cases of public secrets abound in various forms both historically and contemporarily in various human settings. Obviously, the cases discussed are in a broader sense than what is usually understood as "cases" in the arena of scholarship. The selected cases involve Chinese history, a governmental agency, U.S. business, and even a fable. By including cases of such a great variety, I intend to illustrate the ubiquity of the communication phenomenon of public secrets. I included the Danish writer Andersen's famous fable of "the King's New Clothes" because I believe the realistic, camera-type reflection of reality may not always be the best reflection of the genuine reality. Nonacademic literature, including literary literature, can be a richer and more condensed form of reflection of reality.

Two stories from Chinese history are of good illustration of public secrets. The first story tells about how an ancient Chinese king singled out people that might go against him. He had a deer put in the courtyard and summoned all his high officials into this courtyard. The king then claimed, "I believe that the animal standing here is a horse. What do you think? I need an individual answer from each of you." All the officials individually gave his own answer. What finally turned out was that all those who insisted that the animal was not a horse but a deer were executed. From then on, the sole standard for "truth" in the court was the word of the king, and the officials reported not from what they knew but from what they believed was safe. This story illustrates that fear can turn what everyone clearly knows into an unexpressible and buried secret. Gradually, what is not expressed is not recognized as a part of knowledge and thus not a part of facts and reality (Butterfield, 1990).

Another story, also from Chinese history, describes how the new governor Ximenbao effected good order into the County of Ye by practicing the concocted "truth" upon those "truth" manufacturers. The County of Ye was suffering from a major drought. All crops were failing. Incumbent officials saw a golden chance in this drought to extract a fortune from the masses for the purpose of fattening their own personal pockets. They stipulated that all people of the County pay monetary tributes to the God of the River to appease this God's anger which, according to these officials, was apparently manifested in the current drought, and that beautiful girls also should be sacked and put into the river as sacrifice and bribery to the God of the River. All those who refused to believe the officials' logic or to follow their stipulation were severely punished. Bad government put the County in sustained disarray and poverty. Everyone knew that all the monetary tributes went into the personal pockets of the officials and that the beautiful girls were drowned in the river, yet this knowledge was not publicly expressed within the County. However, complaints gradually found their way into the ears of higher officials.

A new governor Ximenbao was sent to the County to redress the complaints that were in secret circulation. After getting to know what was really going on in the County of Ye, Ximenbao decided to use the corrupted officials' logic on the officials themselves. He said, "Existing strategies obviously don't work because people in this County are still suffering from drought and poverty, which is evident in the continued manifestation of the River God's anger. This God probably doesn't like young girls. He likes people with money and power. You officials fit this category and should be sacked and put into the river." And Ximen-bao did what he said. Under this new governor's leadership, people's life in the County of Ye drastically improved.

This story, like the first one, illustrates how fear of penalty plays a role in the production of public secrets. Additionally, this story suggests that one strategy to deal with public secrets is to practice the logic and mechanism that prevent the sharable knowledge in public secrets from becoming the actionable knowledge to guide policy formulation, upon the very producer of this logic and mechanism.

We all know the famous fable "the King's New Clothes," by the Danish writer Andersen. This story wonderfully illustrates how public secrets can blatantly exist against common logic and popular knowledge. In the story, everyone, including the bystanders, the king himself, and of course the imposters, knows with his/her own eyes that the king is naked, yet no one points out the truth. Consequently, widespread knowledge is not expressed and thus kept secret or tacit. At last, a child shouts out the truth. Why do all the adults consciously distort what they clearly see with their own physical eyes? Why does the king himself accept the foolish make-belief that he is wearing gorgeous silk when he actually knows that he is embarrassingly naked? Why is the child the only one shouting out the truth? All the answers have to do with understanding the motivation or causes of public secrets. In this case, protection of one's good "image" by not being perceived as a fool motivates all the adults to lie against their own eyes and private consciousness. Lying by a mass of people also makes individual lying easier and frequently the individual's passport into the group's membership. All this framework of psychology is absent in the little kid who works from his actual, intuitive perception that he acquires from his own eyes.

The effort to maintain a good public image is a powerful cause of public secrets. The management and leadership of many organizations deliberately and even arduously suppress and/or distort information in order to protect the image of themselves or the image of the organization. This effort may be attributed to ideological reasons, yet as a consequence of this effort, information known to one group of organization members is kept secret to another group. This configuration of information distribution is often laden with risks, causing even disasters like what happened in the tragedy of the Space Shuttle Challenger.

On January 28, 1986, the Space Shuttle Challenger exploded 72 seconds after launch from Cape Canaveral, killing the seven crew members on board. A presidential blue ribbon commission, headed by former Secretary of State William Rogers, investigated the accident and produced an exhaustive final report big and heavy enough to use as a doorstep. The root cause of the disaster, so costly in human and financial terms, was not technical but communicational. Essential information, though known by many engineers, was deliberately kept secret from other key personnel involved in the project (Dettmer, 1998).

NASA, in order to keep cost low or a good image of efficiency, accepted Morton Thickol's bid for SRB (Solid Rocket Booster), a key component of the Space Shuttle. Later, it was found that Morton Thickol's SRB could not be expected to keep up to its designed function in a low temperature launch. Major engineers of Morton Thickol clearly knew this. Yet to build a new SRB from scratch would be very expensive. Then NASA reclassified the aft field point, which is the home of the SRB, as "critical," meaning loss of life and vehicle if the SRB failed. Yet this reclassification was not communicated and kept secret from other personnel involved in the project, who, as a result, possessed no information needed to pose rational objection to launches in low temperatures. NASA covered up this crucial information in an effort to avoid any delay of the planned launch on January 28, 1986, and to protect NASA's image of efficiency in the public eye (Dettmer, 1998).

Shortly before the launch, the temperature was 37 degrees Fahrenheit, which was below the safe launch temperature of 53 degrees Fahrenheit (And this safe temperature value is for a shuttle with well-functioning SRB). Morton Thickol engineers vigorously opposed the launch. NASA shuttle managers "shouted down" the opposition of Morton Thickol engineers and Morton Thickol Vice-President over-ruled his own engineers. Depending on their past success in surviving this kind of risk, NASA managers believed they could make it again and keep intact their image of efficiency and economy. Space Shuttle Challenger was launched 11:38 AM EST. Seven-tenths of a second after the actual launch, an exceptional amount of hot exhaust gas blew out of the aft field joint, where the dysfunctional SRB sat. Challenger's main fuel tank exploded 72 seconds into flight. Challenger was destroyed. All the seven crew members were killed. It took NASA nine years and billions of dollars to build the Space Shuttle Challenger (Dettmer, 1998). The Challenger disaster illustrates how costly public secrets can be.

The problem involved in the Mercury Corporation's effort to develop new products can also help illustrate the communication phenomenon of public secrets and how this phenomenon impacts organizational health in a negative way.

The case comes from Argyris and Schön (1996). The Mercury Corporation was established in the 1920s around a single chemical product. With the development of new business in many different fields, Mercury had grown to over three billion dollars in sales by the mid-1960s. As time went on, top management had two concerns. First, their Research and Development Division was not generating new products as quickly as it used to do. Second, the testing and commercialization of new products were meeting with resistance from existing divisions in Mercury.

To alleviate its concerns, Mercury decided and established a New Business Division (NBD) which was empowered not only to develop but also to "incubate" new products. The NBD would turn new products over to existing divisions of Mercury only after it proved that the new products were marketable and profitable.

A new problem arose. By the mid-1970s, after ten years of accumulated experience and a total expenditure of $20 million on research and development, the NBD had failed to produce a single new business of any consequence. As the favorite son of the top management, the NBD was not criticized and allowed to remain in being. However, the staff of the NBD themselves got uneasy. The management of the NBD was puzzled as to what exactly was going wrong. The management of the NBD called in an outside consultant.

The external consultant decided to begin by listening to the "story" of every relevant person. Although people were initially rather taciturn, they gradually opened up. Everyone's story was not exactly the same, but two revelations slowly emerged. One, there were undercurrent common themes among different stories. Two, the stories, when put together as a complementary whole, made a lot of sense in helping to understand and visualize the "map" of the NBD problem. The "map" of the problem and how the consultant helped solve the problem will not be discussed (for details in this regard, reference may be made to Argyris and Schön, 1996, pp. 52–72). The case is intended to show how public secrets exist and impact organizational health.

The external consultant asked the NBD staff whether they had ever told their "stories" before. They informed the consultant that they, as individuals, expressed their views in private, with family, friends or some colleagues. They never publicly confronted each other with their views and understandings in such situations as conferences. Everyone already had knowledge or at least a piece of knowledge about what was going wrong. Many staff members, through their private interactions, realized that they shared much consensus in their private knowledge and understandings, yet they felt hesitant to publicly express their knowledge and views because they felt that problems were to be buried rather than exhumed.

So the little pieces that combine to build up the "map" of the problem were already existent within the NBD staff, yet the pieces remained latent, hidden, tacit, private, disconnected in the form of public secrets. The inability to transform those public secrets into "actionable knowledge" cost Mercury $20 million and its NBD 10 years. The mere existence of knowledge in people's minds does not create value for an organization. Only knowledge in action does that. The tacit knowledge in people's mind must be publicized and transferred into repositories like organizational documents so that explicit knowledge becomes widely and officially available, so that sharable knowledge becomes actionable knowledge in order to be able to guide organizational actions.

After a more concrete picture of public secrets facilitated by case illustrations, the next section offers a preliminary discussion of how public secrets impact organizational operation and health.

PRELIMINARY DISCUSSION OF CONSEQUENCES OF PUBLIC SECRETS

The preface introduced this study's five research questions. And now the reader may question why I do a preliminary discussion only of the issue of consequences of public secrets before the actual study. The reason is that it is exactly the issue or my understanding of the consequences of public secrets that prompted this study. This may already have been manifest in the preface. Also, I perceive a preliminary discussion of possible consequences of public secrets as a rationale for the study.

One negative result that public secrets may lead to is what will be referred to as "bad economy of communication." Public secrets necessitate communicative euphemism, indirect communication, or communication through subtle channels, and perhaps, worst of all, a culture of secrecy.

The basic idea of communication economy is that necessary information should be transmitted to its desired target for the quickest and most accurate reception possible. One manifestation of bad communication economy is information distortion. According to Carley and Lin (1997), there are five sources of information distortion: missing information, incorrect information, agent unavailability, communication channel breakdowns, and agent turnover. Public secrets may contribute to the first four sources of information distortion. The dichotomy of public secrets indicates that information available in one communication context is usually missing in another communication context. Genuine information expressed and exchanged in one communication context may be changed or distorted in another communication context, contributing to incorrect information in the latter context. Communication channel breakdowns and unavailability of official information from official agents are among obvious causes of public secrets.

The public side of public secrets indicates that public secrets contain existent, known, and shared information in one communication channel. The secret side of "public secrets," on the other hand, indicates that information contained in the public secrets fails to enter or is refused recognition in another communication channel. Thus information that is existent and known in one channel is covered in another. As a result, sharable knowledge contained in public secrets fails to become actionable knowledge, knowledge that guides public and explicit actions of an organization and its members. The awkward result is that people who are able to make effective use of the information (i.e., people in authority) fail to use the information, mostly because of their lack of knowledge of such information; people who are not in the authority positions, and thus not able to transform essential information into organizational actions, possess the information. In the case of the Challenger disaster, essential information was kept secret to key personnel who were in the position to make crucial decisions about the design and launch of the space shuttle. How could these people not make serious mistakes?

In many cultures, efficiency and good communication economy dictate that direct communication is better than indirect communication; that public communication is better than covert communication. This is so because the direct and public method takes less time and involves less complication than the indirect and covert method. Frequently, when the target refuses to recognize the message, the sender of the message, in order to get an issue settled, will send it again and again. If the target refuses to recognize the message in one form, the sender will send it in another form. Sometimes, the target may learn to refuse the message in as many forms as possible, the sender then has to learn new and even unusual communication forms to send the message in order to get a certain issue settled. This whole process of learning to refuse and send the same message in various forms in order to either avoid or produce the desired effect costs an organization greatly in many terms, financially, temporally, and psychologically.

In Chinese history, for example, court officials used to employ fables, innuendoes, stories, and analogies in an effort to suggest strategies to the king and to redress mistaken policies. These officials employed such a strategy instead of directly addressing the relevant issues because a frontal presentation or discussion of salient problems may incur personal dangers and even disasters. Consequently, communication between the king and the officials may never have produced the result desired by the court officials. On one hand, the king could always pretend that the officials were trying to amuse him by telling stories and fables, or by sporting literary talent and logic games. On the other hand, the officials found it inadvisable to refute the king's pretense by saying, for example, "No, your majesty, I'm actually criticizing you." With this subtle mechanism going on, glaring problems remained unaddressed despite widespread knowledge of their causes.

The bad economy of communication causes vast amounts of waste in human and material resources.

The usual case of public secrets is that general organization members keep their known and existing information secret from authority figures. Yet the reverse case can also happen. Authority figures keep existent and understood information secret or tacit to non-authority figures. This latter case of public secrets also causes bad communication economy which in turn may lead to disastrous human misery. For illustration, I would like to cite one incident of human misery that occurred in a Chinese city. This case comes from *China News Digest* (or *Hua Xia Wen Zhai,* the original Chinese name), June 23, 1999.

On January 2, 1999, in Linhai City of Zhejiang province, China, a four-year-old girl, Ye Qianqian fell off a second story balcony. Her dad rushed her into Taizhou hospital nearby. The doctor asked the dad to wait and did a CT photo of the girl's brain. After looking at the CT photo, the doctor told the dad that there was nothing serious and that they should go home. After arrival at home, clear symptoms from the girl told the dad that she was dying. Early the next morning, the dad rushed his four-year-old to the hospital again. He had run all about the hospital trying desperately to locate an available doctor to have a look at his dying daughter. By midnight January 3, one doctor came only to tell this dad that his daughter's pupils had dilated and the girl was dying. If he let his daughter stay and die inside the hospital, she would get cremated. The sorrow-stricken dad absolutely did not want to do this to his dying four-year-old daughter. The girl died soon after arriving home. This grieved dad could not figure out what had gone wrong. He innocently believed that doctors are naturally obligated to save life unconditionally. What he did not know was that, as many friends suggested to him later, the doctor expected a "red bag" (containing money as bribery). This naïve dad did not know that this practice has become widely though taciturnly accepted in numerous places (including hospitals) in China. He went only with what was officially communicated and documented and he made a serious mistake (Pan, 1999). The result of tacit information which is not publicly explicit is not only human misery, but also devastation of an institution's image.

Many practices within numerous organizations are not officially communicated to the public, but the organization members are expected to know them. Ignorance of these covert or tacit practices may cause the involved person a myriad of troubles and even disasters such as what happened to the poor dad and his four-year-old girl. Such a communication situation is very bad economy and causes great waste, confusion, and diffidence; the organization members can never be sure how exactly they should act in order not to offend and be effective at the same time. Mind-reading, another economically costly practice in communication, is something organization members have to learn to function well in a culture of secrecy. In many workplaces, "effective" communication, unfortunately, is still largely determined by one's ability to guess what goes on in the mind of the boss.

Acquiring communicative ability in many organizational cultures is a costly task. What informs people best is not the explicit and the written, but the implicit and the unwritten that can only be learned through subtle interpersonal interactions. The bulk of communication knowledge reveals itself only through one's trials, mistakes, and successes. The organization member needs to try different strategies and see which one works. Select those successful strategies and accumulate; the faster one does this, the faster one acquires communicative competence. This trial and test process of learning communicative competence is time-consuming and psychologically debilitating. Since it is all done and fulfilled with great indirectness and subtlety, mistakes are easily made, hearts are cavalierly broken, faces are mysteriously lost and saved, and confusion is widely distributed. The phenomenon of public secrets teaches people to invest more time in studying interactive skills rather than in solving problems, many of which themselves are public secrets.

The existence of public secrets also teaches people that something, though public among one group of people or in one communication context, is still and should remain a secret or a taboo with another group of people (frequently people in power) or in another communication context. Therefore, communication about necessary topics with the latter group of people or in the latter communication context becomes dangerous, a matter that needs to be managed with great finesse. As a result, innuendo becomes a common practice in these organizations. This practice, as illustrated in the discussion of ancient Chinese officials' communication strategy with the king, leads to very inefficient communication.

The practice of innuendo leads to wasteful communication because of loose interpretability and rich ambiguity. All innuendoes can be interpreted at least in two senses, denotatively and connotatively. Although innuendoes are effective in avoiding immediate harm and in saving faces, innuendoes often fail to fulfill their intended task because the message sender uses the connotative meaning, but the message receiver uses the denotative meaning. Consequently, the message sender and the message receiver communicate totally *past* each other instead of *with* each other. What the message sender intends as serious discussion may only turn out, to the message receiver, as literary, anecdotal, or artistic display or entertainment. This communication *past* each other instead of *with* each other wastes vast amounts of time, human effort and talent. Investment into communication does not go to what to communicate but how to communicate, which can prove much more demanding and time-consuming than "what to communicate." If the claim is true that one can only acquire personal and public integrity by squaring inner thought with outward behavior, the phenomenon and climate of public secrets may make personal and public integrity extremely difficult. Public secrets do not contribute to personal and public integrity; they contribute to social schizophrenia.

The organizational communication phenomenon of public secrets may be psychologically damaging to general organization members. Many of organization members' understandings, feelings, conceptions about organizational problems and improvements exist in the form of public secrets because of these members' deprived ability or opportunity to publicly express their information. Yet the information in these public secrets is absent in the knowledge repository for the organization's decision-making process and fails to be incorporated into the organization's formulation of policies, regulations, goals, and strategies. Thus, when organizational members act according to those prescribed organizational policies, regulations, goals, and strategies, they may actually act against their own understandings, feelings, and conceptions, or at least they may perceive so. Nothing is perhaps more demotivating and alienating than acting against one's own knowledge and logical consciousness. Performance under such duress over a long time only encourages people to give up using their mental power and perform only with their hands. A popular Chinese saying indicates this sad consequence from the inability to act according to one's own consciousness, "Absence of logical consciousness is a blessing," because the presence of such consciousness only causes cognitive dissonance which in turn leads to psychological discomfort.

The negative psychological implications from the phenomenon of public secrets are numerous. The existence of such phenomenon insinuates to general organization members that something is "undiscussable" in public or official situations. The feeling that there are things undiscussable causes general fear, confusion, hesitance, diffidence, and, worst of all, a culture of secrecy. People may become very uncertain about how they should rein their mouths and even their minds. This uncertainty in turn breeds a feeling of insecurity. Athanassiades (1973) argues that insecurity is a major breeder of information distortion. Information distortion is anti-learning because it creates false realities. Actions according to false realities will only lead the organization into danger. For the sake of clarity, I'd like to briefly digress and mention the distinction between rumors and information distortion since much conventional wisdom take rumors as one form of information distortion. As I argued previously in this chapter by citing research literature, rumors frequently represent expression, in the informal organizational communication context, of spontaneous or credible information whose expression in the formal context is somewhat suppressed. Information distortion, however, is a deliberate alteration or cover-up of information. If the reader equates rumors with information distortion, which does not reflect my understanding, the reader will easily be puzzled by an apparent contradiction between my present contention against information distortion and my previous contention in favor of "rumors" or the grapevine. My brief digression here is to help clear up this possible confusion.

The phenomenon of public secrets represents a dichotomous oxymoron which in turn comes from an existence of dual communication systems within the organization, the official and the unofficial communications. Yet public secrets do not indicate a peaceful but an antagonistic co-existence of these two communication systems. This antagonistic co-existence of dual communication systems leads to a rift between the general organization members and the organization's decision-makers. The "*we-they*" mentality is a major symptom of this rift. Such a rift costs the organization dearly, though in hard-to-measure manners, because this rift produces distrust, which in turn produces the need for inspection, which in turn necessitates human and material resources to be devoted to the non-productive or even counter-productive inspection. The basic assumption underlying a lot of inspection is that people are not to be trusted; that is why they need to be closely inspected. According to the communication theory of self-fulfilling prophecy, people not trusted gradually become, in reality (or at least in perception), distrustful and untrustworthy. What I mean is that the dual communication systems as reflected in and strengthened by the phenomenon of public secrets tend to produce a vicious cycle, which, once in session, will entail a Herculean effort to halt. Liu (1986) explains at length the negative impact (especially that of distrust) that the existence of dual communication systems in China causes upon general morale in the nation. And he provides a diagram of the two systems which can help us understand the various media within the formal-institutionalized and the informal-noninstitutionalized communication systems (please refer to figure 1.2).

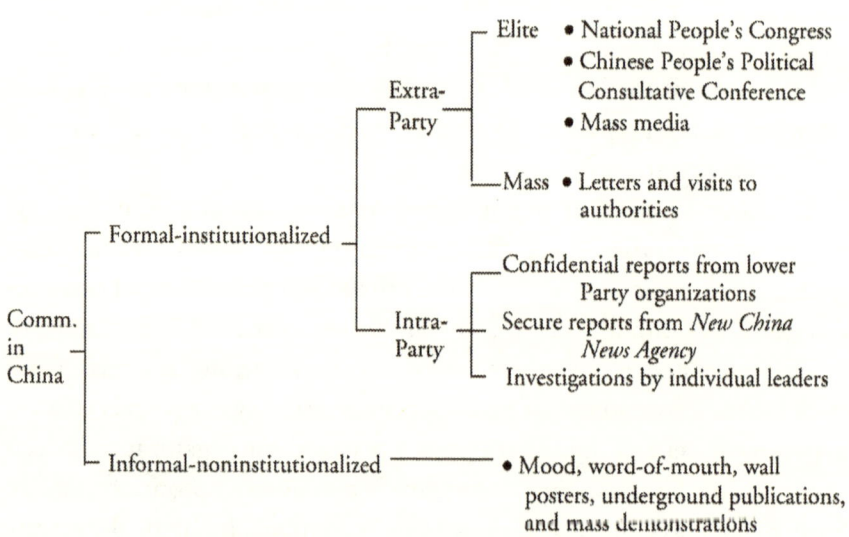

Figure 1.2 Dual Communication Systems in China
(From page 263 of Liu's *How China Is Ruled*)

Distrust contributes to a defensive organizational communication climate. According to Gibb (1961), increases in defensive behavior were positively correlated with losses in communication efficiency, particularly information or communication distortion. In a defensive communication climate, it will be hard to know how much time and resources people expend for the purpose of defending or justifying themselves, covering up mistakes and problems, and evading the substantial by laboring the superficial. All this non-productive hustle and bustle will rob the organization of precious amounts of energy that could be channeled into profit and quality of work life. Protective lying frequently goes hand in hand with a defensive communication climate.

When people lie, they surely say what they do not mean. According to one Chinese sage (probably Laotzu), if what is said is not what is meant, what ought to be done remains undone; if what ought to be done remains undone, morals and art are corrupted; if morals and art are corrupted, justice will go astray, and the people will stand about in helpless confusion.

I do not intend to go into all those rippling implications from the evil root of public secrets as orated by the Chinese sage. I would argue that at least one other negative implication can emerge from the existence of public secrets: the agenda of mediocrity. Failure to transform public secrets into actionable knowledge will lead to what I call the agenda of mediocrity. Without being able to channel their knowledge, understanding, and information into the official communication line or into actionable knowledge, organization members easily perceive that they are not responding to the relevant (what they conceive needs to be done), but to the irrelevant (what they are told to do). This perception is perhaps the biggest killer of intrinsic motivation. This perception often represents what occurs in reality.

General organization members, especially frontline people, because of their proximity to daily organizational reality, usually possess important knowledge and information. Without the integral part of the organizational communication system composed of general organization members, many diagnostic conclusions of the organization can be wrong. As a result, the organization might well labor the irrelevant while the relevant is left untouched. The unresolved problem that remains will only lead the management and leadership into the syndrome of "what we need is a bigger hammer." The irony is that the harder the hammer falls upon the irrelevant, the harder the problem backfires with more severity, as explained by Senge (1990). Another vicious cycle is ready to plague the organization. The more severe the problem becomes, the more stringent rules and inspection the management implements, leading to more nonchalant and cynical employees.

One anonymous quotation I read somewhere said, "The thing that really worries business today is the great number of people still on their payroll who are *unemployed*." *Unemployed* here does not mean "out of job." Everyone is still in his/her job, but he/she is not doing his/her job. Or, people are not committed to their jobs. How could they commit themselves to their jobs? They are not allowed to act according to the information or knowledge which they share so widely among themselves. Their information, understanding, and knowledge are only sharable but not actionable. As a result, employees are hired only with their hands, not with their heads, far less with their hearts—they are hired "from their neck down." What a waste of human resources! If Drucker (1993) is correct by saying that information and knowledge have become *the* resource of modern organizations, then many organizations may offer salaries without making much use of their only resource because those organizations do not make use of what is in their people's heads—the only location of informational resources within people. The organizational communication phenomenon of public secrets, before its transformation into actionable, public knowledge, wastes incalculable amounts of human and material resources.

PURPOSE OF STUDY

The purpose of every academic study should be twofold, including an ultimate purpose and an immediate purpose. Clarification of the former helps the researcher keep sight of the connection between his or her work and the final, big picture he or she attempts to achieve. This clarification helps decrease fragmentation in academic studies by connecting specific studies with a unified high-order aim. It also helps make sure that various practical, realistic academic efforts are going toward an idealistic, cooperative, and final terminal. The ultimate purpose provides the motivation for the researcher by countering disillusionment which may be a product of not knowing where one is exactly and ultimately going with his or her studies. On the other hand, every academic study should involve an immediate purpose. Clarification of the immediate purpose helps the researcher keep sight of his or her practical agenda, what he or she specifically wants to achieve through every specific study. A high purpose without a practical agenda may well lead to an ideal that lacks practical steps for its fulfillment.

The ultimate purpose of this research project is greater civility within and civilization of the workplace. There is no perfect civilization on the planet. Different places are only of different degrees of civilization. My personal yardstick for measuring the degree of civilization is the discrepancy between individual logic and communal logic. By "individual logic" I mean the logic that people use in their quiet privacy. By "communal logic," I mean the communally approved logic that people use in public or in an organized group. The less the discrepancy between individual logic and communal logic within a human location, the more civilized the location is. This personal yardstick is based on what I have acquired from all my interactions (scholarly and non-scholarly) with my world.

In my view, human civilization could have at least three development phases: the mythological freedom, the industrial freedom, and the human freedom. In the mythological freedom phase, people depend on myths for psychological liberation of themselves. Physically, people are not very free in this phase; people lack control over their physical world. This lack of control causes materialistic misery in people's lives. People may not have an adequate and sustained supply of food, shelter, and clothing. To strengthen their sense of control over their lives, people try to compensate by better explanations of their world. Yet, on the other hand, people do not possess enough scientific knowledge to aid their explanation. Consequently, they depend on mythological explanations. Scientific logic (largely absent in this phase) and conscious human struggle (too weak in this phase) fail to help alleviate human misery in the mythological freedom period. The only path to freedom, freedom only in psychological terms, is found in total submission to mythology. Private, individual logic is largely absent in this phase of human development.

In the industrial freedom phase, technology enables people to enjoy freedom from physical restraints imposed by their environment. For example, the air-conditioner gives people freedom from the unpleasant summer heat. Yet in the industrial freedom phase, much human misery comes not from materialistic poverty, but from poverty in the design of human organizations. Lack of knowledge and resources in poorly designed human organizations force individual organization members to subject their private, individual logic to the organization's communal logic with the consequence of compromising and sacrificing their individual initiative and creativity. This subjection causes "interactional" misery, misery on and by people because of their own improper organization of themselves. In the phase of industrial freedom, organizations still lack capacity to accommodate their members' individuality, initiative, and creativity. Private, individual logic is largely suppressed in this phase.

In the human freedom phase, people enjoy freedom from both the restraints of the physical world and the inadequacy of poorly designed human organizations. The precondition for this phase is rational and rich design of human organizations so that they are highly accommodative of individuality. An organization that promises human freedom has adequate knowledge and resources to accommodate its members' individual initiatives. These resources not only come from technological advances, but, more importantly, from application of rich human knowledge. The industrial freedom phase has, as its defining feature, standardization, whose uppermost purpose is efficient production of materialistic wealth. Materialistic wealth is *the* product of the industrial freedom phase. The phase of human freedom, however, has, as its defining feature, *accommodation,* whose uppermost purpose is exploration and exploitation of individual logic, initiative, creativity, and wellbeing. Materialistic wealth is the *by*-product of this phase. Private, individual logic is largely freed in this phase of human freedom.

Ultimately, I hope my research contributes toward the advent and/ or growth of the human freedom phase through truer expression and better understanding of the private, individual logic; by decreasing the discrepancy between private, individual logic and communal, organizational logic; and through fuller exploration and exploitation of the private, individual logic.

To come down from the clouds of idealism onto the earth of realism, the immediate purpose of my research project is to search for a better understanding of the organizational communication phenomenon of public secrets and for tactics and strategies to transform the sharable knowledge within public secrets into actionable knowledge for the purpose of better organizational health and better quality of work and work life by and for organizational members.

The tension between individuality and collectivity is one of the basic roots of organizational conflicts. Countless scholarly efforts have been made to bridge the gap. Scholars of leadership and organizational behavior (e.g., Bennis, 1985, 1989; Covey, 1991, 1993a, 1993b, 1994; Deming, 1986, 1993; Drucker, 1986, 1988, 1993; Herzberg, 1968, 1973, 1992; O'Toole, 1996; Rost, 1993; Senge, 1990), for example, generally agree that a successful organization must learn to accommodate individuality into its organizational goal. One basic leadership capability, according to these scholars, is to draw out true individuality from organizational members and extract, from these members' individualities, inclusive and high-order guiding principles that are truest possible representation of the broadest range of individual wishes.

Yet scholars have not given enough attention to the major location where individualism is most truly manifested—the organization's informal communication context. Most organizational studies only address members' actions, including their communication actions, in the institutionalized context. Topics in organizational communication, including scientific management, human relations theory, interpersonal communication, group communication, intra-organizational communication, and inter-organizational communication, all are largely researched in organization members' work or institutionalized interactional context, but not in their life or informal context.

Congruence between work and life is perhaps largely existent only with young children. This congruence is, to a great extent, absent with the majority of adults. To acquire a better understanding of problems in human organizations, researchers must go beyond the formal, institutionalized communication scene or beyond the communal logic, and go into the organization's informal/noninstitutionalized communication scene and explore what occurs with organization members' private logic. Direct comparison and contrast between these two scenes is more promising and fruitful than study of only one scene in the effort to improve organizational health. Only by looking at both the private logic and the communal logic can researchers find discrepancy between these two and directly address this discrepancy.

The nature of work as an innate, essential human need must be restored. Work as an integral part of life, not as an unavoidable evil of livelihood, must be restored. For this purpose, we must study why, within the work context, genuine communication and information occur in one channel, but not in another channel. What are those elements in one channel that enable genuine communication and information? How can these elements be transferred into the other channel, usually the organization's formal/official communication channel? What are those elements in the other channel that disable genuine communication and information? How can these elements be alleviated? Public secrets is an interesting and promising departure point to work toward more civility in and civilization of the workplace.

2

LITERATURE REVIEW

LACK OF DIRECT LITERATURE ON RESEARCH OF PUBLIC SECRETS

Regarding research literature on public secrets, I met with great diffi-culty locating it. First of all, the phrase of "public secrets" did not seem to exist in the field of organizational communication. My search revealed that there was virtually no direct literature on the organiza-tional communication phenomenon of "public secrets." Then I tried other terms that, to my logic, may have possible connection with "pub-lic secrets." I searched for "defensive communication" and found Jack R. Gibb. I searched for "information distortion," "message distortion," and "communication distortion," and came across one or two articles. I searched for "lying" and came up with a book that has little to do with my "public secrets." Then I changed my strategy and tried broader terms like "organizational communication" or "organizational behav-ior." To my great pleasure and dismay, I came up with too much to have any clue. I physically went to the shelves where books on organi-zational communication and behavior are located. I thumbed through a good proportion of those books whose names contained some lure to me. No "public secrets." I resignedly went off with something on grapevine and informal communication within the organization. I also have been rummaging through long bibliographies on organizational communication in an effort to find anything that is somewhat connected with "public secrets." More results emerged, but not as much as I wished. Very recently, I realized, through kind advice from a professor, that a book is published on public secrets in mass media in China. This is good news to me. Yet a smooth connection from this book to my study is not easy, since study for this project is set in the organizational context. Of course, my future research on public secrets can branch out into different contexts of public secrets, including that of mass media.

The conclusion I derive from my search for literature on public secrets, which may not have been comprehensive enough, is that public secrets, as an interesting and significant organizational communication phenomenon, is not yet very much recognized by scholars of organizational communication as an issue of itself, though rare pieces with scant relevance to this issue are scattered in organizational communication literature. Yet when I talk with people about the phenomenon I define as public secrets, they all echo with much interest, understanding, and acknowledgement of this phenomenon. Thus I seem to possess reason to say that the organizational communication phenomenon of public secrets is a widespread and significant one to which organizational communication scholars haven't given adequate attention.

In this section I would like to walk through what I have procured from my search that I believe is relevant to the research of public secrets and explain, at proper places, the heuristic value, the inspiration, and the implications the collected literature may have for the research of public secrets. I categorize the collected literature in the following areas (roughly in such an order—from the more theoretical to the more applied, from the most pertinent to the less pertinent): (1) systems theory in the context of organizational studies; (2) dichotomies in the organization; (3) the cultural phenomenon of taboo; (4) defensive communication and information distortion; (5) the learning organization; and (6) communication, motivation, and organizational health.

SYSTEMS THEORY IN THE CONTEXT OF ORGANIZATIONAL STUDIES

The phenomenon of public secrets may signal a dysfunctional communication system within an organization in that public secrets create a dichotomy and rift in the organization's communication system, and thus evidences a lack of congruence among different components of the organization.

The general systems theory is a highly inclusive and comprehensive philosophical framework. This highly heuristic theory may acquire different "faces" when applied to different human studies. Different aspects of the general systems theory are accentuated for better explanations of different characteristics of different systems. Surely I cannot get the totality of the general systems theory straight within a brief review. For the purpose of this work, I would emphasize the implications of the general systems theory when it is applied to the research of organizational communication and studies. Particularly, I will explain the concept of information and atrophy as Bertalanffy (1951, 1952, 1968, 1975, 1981), the founding father of the general systems theory, interpreted. This may help illustrate the relationship between organizational information (as manifested in the phenomenon of public secrets in terms of this research) and organizational health or deterioration.

There are four important implications of the general systems theory for organizational analysis and organizational information processing.[1]

The first implication is interdependence. Interdependence both occurs intra-organizationally and inter-organizationally. Interdependence is a combined concept from dependence and independence. Within the systemically functioning organization, all organizational members and components are first independent. They all have their own unique task to fulfill in their own unique location with their own unique local conditions. If an element is not so, it is redundant and

---

1.   Unless specified, review in this section is of the works of Bertalanffy.

should be excised from the systemic body of the organization to avoid waste. The uniqueness of every organizational element entitles it a right to autonomy, a role and equal importance in information processing. It's easy to imagine what happens if the head one day decides that the information sent by the tongue is not as important as the information sent by the eye. Organizational elements or members not only should enjoy a right to share their unique information, they should also be given latitude to make use of this information with discretion. Imagine again what would happen if one local area on the human body is infected and does not take any immediate disinfectant actions while waiting for the "official order from the top."

The other side of interdependence is dependence. Dependence means that every organizational member has to depend on others in order to successfully carry out his/her own role and responsibility. Coordination, an indispensable condition for the complicated modern organization, is, more than anything else, based on organizational members' dependence on each other. The network of dependence dictates that mistake by one organizational department may vibrate its negative effect throughout the entire organization. Therefore the quality of information from various organizational members is equally important. Blocking of information to some organizational members is not facilitating administrative control over and creating order within the organization, but forcing those information-deprived members to make mistakes, mostly in an unconscious and imperceptible manner. These members' mistakes are not their own mistakes only (though they are frequently so accused), the mistakes are the whole organization's mistakes. Suppose what the organizational statistician receives is but wrongly reported or even deliberately distorted numbers, the report he/she submits will accordingly become invalid. Working from invalid financial conclusions, decision-making agents will not be able to formulate wise directions to various organizational departments. Working from ill-advised directions, organizational members will not be able to execute effective actions. The cycle may go on and on, with further rounds of the cycle causing further damage to organizational effectiveness. In modern organizations where streamlined operations involve complicated, interlocked steps, mutual dependence may either lead to greater success or greater disasters.

For healthy organizational functioning, organizational members should both be independent and dependent or interdependent so that valid information not only exists but is also shared and exploited, so that organizational members are both contributive and cooperative.

The second implication of the general systems theory when applied to human organizations is openness. Openness means that every organization is open to its internal and external environments. No organization is self-dependent, self-contained, or self-sufficient. No organization, as with every person, is a "solitary island." The organization constantly depends on its environment for its input, including raw materials, parts from other manufacturers, customers' needs, and the market. Actually without their environment, organizations will not even be able to find a purpose for their own existence. Organizations strive hard every day mostly for the single purpose of obtaining more successful interactions with its environment. How successfully the organization carries out its interactions with the environment depends on how well the organization knows about this environment, which in turn depends on how much valid information the organization collects and maintains about this environment. Without an informational basis, the organization's interactions with its environment will be like "shooting in the dark." In this sense, those organizational members who have the greatest amount of contact with the environment, or the "environment-spanners," acquire conspicuous importance in the organization's information processing. The majority of the environment-spanners are the frontline people, including both the frontline employees and the frontline managers. As Peter Drucker (1993) contends, in the new information-based organizations that are presently evolving, knowledge and expertise will be primarily distributed at the bottom, held by those who have the most direct contact with the environment and the customers.

Microscopic and macroscopic analytic framework is the third implication the general systems theory has upon organizational communication. Put simply, there are different levels within an organization. The organization is composed of many smaller organizations. A number of organizations on this level combine to build up the organization of a higher level. The organization is an organization of organizations. Microscopically, every element within the organization is a system of its own. This element has its own worries, aspirations, problems, and agenda, whether this element is a person or department. Macroscopically, the organization itself is but one member of its environment. Membership becomes an important issue in organizational unity and integration. This membership is more than anything else built upon an access to adequate information. Without information, there will not be knowledge and familiarity with the group to which one nominally belongs. Without knowledge and familiarity, there will not be a sense of inclusion. Too frequently, organizational members do not know "what is going on at the top or in the middle." Yet these members are under daily exhortation that they should feel as "owners" of the company. It will be extremely difficult for organization members to have a feeling of ownership and inclusion which is guaranteed first of all by adequate access to information.

The fourth implication of the general systems theory in the context of the organization is the concept of organizational adaptation and innovation. This is closely connected with the previous implication of openness. Since organizations are open to their environment, they are then open to all influences from this environment. Ignoring these influences may endanger the very survival of the organization. What is more important, the environment is more fickle than ever before in this post-industrial or informational age. Adaptations to environmental changes must be made and made accurately and promptly. Accurate, constant, and prompt adaptations have long evolved to become a habit in various aspects of human life. When the sunlight is strong, for example, the eyes quickly squint or shut. Well, they may refuse to shut for the purpose of experimenting with an unpleasant physical feeling.

One big problem with organizational adaptation lies in the speed with which this adaptation is made. An adaptation made too late is no longer an adaptation but a meaningless action. An adaptation made in time is reaction. An adaptation made in advance by anticipation of environmental changes is proaction. Proaction is the best, offering the organization the ease of poised preparation. Reaction is next, offering the organization passive following of external forces. Meaningless action because of belated adaptation is the worst, offering the organization nothing but panting exhaustion, waste, and atrophy. When an organization is proactive, it is innovative. Innovation often results in phenomenal organizational success. Whether an organization is reactive, proactive, or just wasting its time depends on how quickly and accurately it collects and processes information about its relevant environment. Effective information collecting, processing, and applying must come from an effective information system.

There is one section in Bertalanffy's (1968) General Systems Theory that specifically addresses "information and atrophy." Since the topic of this work is public secrets which, at the base, is a communicational and informational phenomenon, I would like to introduce this section by Bertalanffy.

According to Bertalanffy (1968), energy is the currency of physics, just like economic values can be expressed in dollars and pounds. The flow of information in organizational communication corresponds to the flow of energy in physics. The light bulb is on simply because there is a constant supply of energy—the electrical power. The eye squints in the sunlight because of energy. First, the eye receives the energy emitted in the sunlight. Then the eye reacts by virtue of its muscular energy. In the case of organizational effectiveness, the flow of information carries the energy (like the wire carries electricity) that flows within the organization and between the organization and its environment. Whether an organization rejuvenates or debilitates itself depends on how much energy this organization enjoys—energy that is contained in the flow of information within the organization. The amount and quality of information helps determine the speed and validity of organizational decision-making.

Bertalanffy (1968) offers the example of "the game of Twenty Questions," where people are supposed to finally find an object by receiving, from the experimenter, "yes-no" answers to questions they ask. For example, the people may ask, "Is the thing in the cabinet?" or "Is the thing in the drawer?" The more questions the people ask, the more likely they would find the object. The lesson from this experiment to organizational information processing is that the more questions the organization asks, the more information it receives; the more information it receives, the more likely it will reach valid and successful answers and solutions. Without receiving enough information, the organization actually ignores many existent factors that operate in the environmental reality and thus bases its decision-making upon wrongly perceived reality and even upon fantasy. The problem with many organizations' administrations is still that they give their people more orders than listening sessions. Or there is an imbalance between the downward and upward communications, frequently with the former greatly outweighing the latter. These administrations never seem to be able to understand the simple idea that the purpose for us to have two ears but one mouth is to listen twice as much as we speak. They do not seem to understand that good decisions come from valid, comprehensive information which, in turn, comes from systemic collection. They do not seem to understand that information is the currency of energy for the organization which would fall into atrophy if operating always in a low-power state.

The second concept that Bertalanffy (1968) talked about in this section of the book was "feedback" (please refer to figure 2.1 on the following page). First, a stimulus occurs. Then the receptor receives information about this stimulus. Then, through the "control apparatus," the message produced from the information collected by the receptor is sent to the effector or executor of a certain action (please note that the message that goes into the "control apparatus" may not be the same as the message that comes out of it). After receiving the message, the effector gives a response to the stimulus. In the world of the organism, this whole process may complete itself in a fraction of a second. In the world of the human organization, this process can sometimes take years. Thus no human organization has, up to now, learned so well as to be equal to the organism. The success of the response is based on two things. One, the speed of information transmission. Two, the accuracy of the information. The success of organizational adaptation and innovation is largely based on the effectiveness of this organization's feedback network, otherwise, a stimulus or an external action may be causing great damage to the organization and the organization is taking no action as a response.

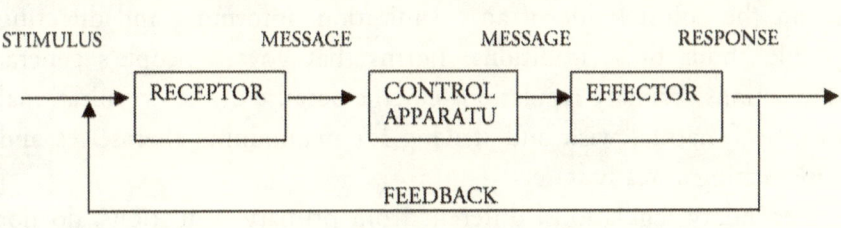

Figure 2.1 Simple Feedback Scheme

Homeostasis, or maintenance of balance in the living organism, as explained by Bertalanffy (1968), is the desired result from successful feedback. Prototypical illustration of homeostasis can be found in the case of the thermo-regulation in warm-blooded animals. These animals maintain a balance with its environment in terms of temperature by promptly and accurately receiving and responding to information they collect through sensing temperature changes in the environment. Misinformation or delay in action will cause a lack of congruence between body temperature and the environmental temperature. When loss of homeostasis occurs, unpleasant physical suffering is inflicted upon the animal. Similarly, an organization will not be able to maintain homeostasis without a constant flow of valid information about the environment and prompt and proper response to this environmental information.

The mechanism that produces homeostasis is what Bertalanffy (1968) called "dynamic interaction," the constantly changing exchanges among organizational elements (p.44). According to Bertalanffy, there are two types of regulations in the system that affect the "dynamic interaction," the primary regulations and the secondary regulations. The primary regulations emerge from the dynamic process of all the interactions among all the organizational members and components. Primary regulations are naturally necessary and tacitly accepted throughout the organization. Primary regulations, it may be said, represent the cultural side of an organization, informing and directing people about those traditional norms that govern people's general interactions. Primary regulations emerge because of the organizational members' natural wish and striving for maintaining themselves and approaching a steady state.

Secondary regulations, different from primary regulations, do not exactly emerge naturally from the natural interactions within an organization. They are rather officially stipulated by the organizational administration. If primary regulations are cultural, then secondary regulations should be administrative. Of course the secondary regulations are frequently formulated on a basis of information that organizational members collect through their formal and professional interactions. Yet this information is administratively categorized, sorted, synthesized, and analyzed for the formal formulation of rules and policies. Administrative feedback scheme can be considered as belonging to the secondary regulations, constituting as a major component of the organization's established, formally announced, administratively maintained communication system. A large number of actual interactions among organizational members are more governed by primary regulations because they are much more dynamic and fluid than the official and formal interactions. These interactions work not exactly in a neat, pre-established framework (Bertalanffy, 1968).

Bertalanffy's distinction between primary and secondary regulations echo Stacey's distinction between the legitimate system and the shadow system within the organization, which I will address later on in this chapter. The interaction between these two regulations, like that between the legitimate and shadow systems, either decreases or increases the phenomenon of "public secrets."

The general systems theory, especially as applied in the context of organizational communication, has much relevance to the research of "public secrets" in that how the system of an organization operates decides how information exists and flows within this organization, which in turn decides how and how much the phenomenon of public secrets exists and operates within this organization.

Additionally, Bertalanffy's (1968) distinction between primary and secondary regulations is helpful in illustrating the fact that there are two information channels in the organization, the official one and the unofficial one. These two channels, when working against each other, may cause serious organizational problems. Public secrets are one manifestation of such organizational problems.

DICHOTOMIES IN THE ORGANIZATION

The organizational communication phenomenon of public secrets, as I explained in the section addressing characteristics of public secrets, is in itself a dichotomous oxymoron. This phenomenon emerges, operates, and prospers because of incongruent interactions between the two polarities of various dichotomies that may be inherent within the organization. Study of the mechanism of various organizational dichotomies will help the understanding of the operation of public secrets.

According to Stacey (1996), an organization is composed of two systems: the legitimate system and the shadow system. The legitimate system "refers to the hierarchy, bureaucracy, and shared ideology that members of an organization recognize as having the authority to sanction actions and allocate resources" (Stacey, 1996, p. 288). Links within the legitimate system are either (1) formally and intentionally established by those organization members in official power or (2) established by well-understood, implicit principles that are widely accepted throughout the organization. These well-understood, implicit principles can be embodied in, for example, a shared culture or accepted ideology. Although the legitimate system is generally predesigned or prescribed before daily organizational operation comes into existence or before other organizational actions are taken, many elements within this system can also evolve with time. The legitimate system is established in order to fulfill the performance of the organization's primary task as believed by those members in official power or by the majority of the members. This primary task is generally, more than anything, the survival of the organization.

What directs the operation of an organization's legitimate system is what Stacey (1996) calls the "dominant schemas." The dominant schemas address the organization's primary tasks and drive its current survival strategies. The dominant schemas are usually embodied in the organization's official artifacts that include rules, regulations, and policies. These dominant schemas are generally prescribed by the organization's official decision-makers. The purpose of the dominant schemas is to give structure, stability, and predictability to the organization. The dominant schemas are also materialized through stipulated official routines like memos, meetings, and reports. We can also say that the dominant schemas operate in structured, stable, and predictable manners.

In the short term, an organization's dominant schemas help decrease the organization's anxiety because they help assure a feeling of structure, stability, and predictability. Yet, in the long term, the dominant schemas actually help increase anxiety for the organization. This is so largely because the prescribed dominant schemas are frequently at clash with reality (both intra-organizational and extra-organizational) which is not and cannot be prescribed and stipulated but is constantly fluid and fickle. This clash between the prescribed dominant schemas and the unprescribed reality eventually leads to maladaptations and hence frustrations and anxiety for the organization (Stacey, 1996).

Organizational learning that occurs within the framework of the legitimate system or the dominant schemas is what Argyris and Schön (1978) would call the single-loop learning or simple learning. Single-loop learning occurs when problems are analyzed into pieces that are intelligible to existent organizational strategies or policies. For the sake of and in order to fit into this intelligibility, additions to, and omissions and distortions of reality may be unconsciously created.

When some parts of a certain problem cannot be rendered intelligible to existent strategies and policies, or when existent strategies and policies cannot solve the problem, single-loop learning may recommend modifications to these strategies and policies. Yet the values and norms or the dominant schemas that are behind those strategies and polices are left intact. Single-loop learning is so called because it is "a single feed-back loop" between reality and organizational strategies and polices.

The shadow system, according to Stacey (1996), refers to the set of interactions among organization members that fall outside the organization's legitimate system. The shadow system includes all social and political interactions that fall outside the rules strictly prescribed by the legitimate system. It is the arena in which organization members pursue their own gain, but also the arena in which they play, create, and prepare innovations. Links within the shadow system are spontaneously and informally established by individual organization members during their multi-dimensional interactions within the organization's legitimate system. The shadow system consists of informal social and political connections among organization members, in which these members develop their own local rules or norms to direct their interactions. The degree to which these rules and norms are shared varies. Sometimes, they are shared only within small groups. Other times, they can even be shared throughout the organization. Yet these rules and norms remain in the shadow in the sense that they do not engage actively in the organization's official operations. The shadow rules and norms constitute a repertoire of organization members' thoughts, perceptions, and behaviors that are potentially available to an organization but are not currently being utilized for its performance of the primary task.

What directs the operation of the shadow system is what Stacey calls the recessive schemas. Recessive schemas refer to the part of an organization's symbol system "that is not being utilized to form the rules driving the system's performance of the current primary task" (Stacey, 1996, p. 289). The recessive schemas are housed in a repertoire of mental contents which either belong to individual organization members or belong to a group of organization members. In other words, the recessive schemas either are not shared with others or are shared within and across some groups, but not widely shared across the organization as a whole, and certainly not utilized as guidelines for organizational actions.

Unlike the organization's dominant schemas, the recessive schemas are not officially prescribed and documented. The recessive schemas are rather fluid, riding the waves of the fickle sea of reality. The recessive schemas flow quite closely with reality as momentary and spontaneous reflections or marks of influence by the reality inside and outside the organization. If the dominant schemas attempt to structure and stabilize reality, the recessive schemas then attempt to mirror reality. Thus, under different influences from different forces, the organization's legitimate system which operates under the dominant schemas is often at "fight" with the organization's shadow system which operates under the recessive schemas.

Organizational learning that occurs outside the framework of the legitimate system or the dominant schemas and with the guidance of the shadow system or the recessive schemas is what Argyris and Schön (1978) would call the double-loop learning. Double-loop learning connects reality or observed effects of action not only with the organization's existent strategies and policies, but also with the values and assumptions or the dominant schemas behind those strategies and policies. Double-loop learning is obviously more inquisitive and thorough than single-loop learning. Double-loop learning is actually so inquisitive that it is often perceived as hostile and destructive by the legitimate system of the organization. This is not surprising because double-loop learning often goes hand in hand with the shadow system or the recessive schemas which is in turn often at odds with the legitimate system or the dominant schemas.

According to Stacey (1996), "the basic dynamics of an organization are determined by the manner in which "the legitimate system and the shadow system interact within an organization" (p. 168). Accordingly, it may also be contended that whether an organization engages in single-loop learning or double-loop learning is also determined by the interaction between these two systems within the organization. Stacey (1996) argues that for an organization to be creative and innovative, there must exist space for novelty within the organization. This space for novelty exists not only when the shadow system is in tension with the legitimate system, but, more importantly, when the shadow system can enter the privileged realm of the legitimate system and thus acquires the potential for modifying and even replacing the legitimate system.

An organization possesses space for creativity, Stacy (1996) contends, when it operates "at the edge of chaos" which, in turn, is primarily determined by the state of the organization's shadow system. The shadow system must be in a state of flux behind the stable façade of the legitimate system. The shadow system must be working to undermine and even disintegrate the legitimate system in acts of creative destruction. When the organization operates in the space for creativity at the edge of chaos, at least some organization members engage in exploratory dialogue, possessing and processing genuine information, and doing self-reflection to develop new knowledge. This new knowledge is first expressed informally or privately within the shadow system as modification or replacement of the organization's recessive schemas. Yet for potential innovations to occur, the expression of this new knowledge must then be amplified into the organization's legitimate system and thus becomes modification and replacement of the organization's dominant schemas (Stacey, 1996).

The organizational communication phenomenon of public secrets, being a dichotomy in itself, also bespeaks of the dichotomy between the organization's legitimate system and its shadow system. The public side of public secrets usually exists and operates in the shadow system; the secret side of public secrets usually exists and operates in the legitimate system. How an organization's legitimate system interacts with its shadow system determines how the secret side of public secrets interacts with the public side of public secrets, how much is partitioned respectively into the secret and public sides of public secrets, and whether the sharable knowledge within public secrets will remain only sharable or will acquire the potential transformation into actable knowledge. For instance, general members within an organization may harbor complaints against a certain organizational policy that favors only the administration. These complaints may go around only informally among colleagues (the shadow system). When it comes to formal occasions like conferences (the legitimate system) where the administration is present, these complaints usually remain quiet or hidden. How likely these complaints will surface as public knowledge in the presence of the administration depends on how thick the "wall" is between the administration and the general employees. How widely these complaints are known and how widely they remain unknown depends on how large the employee body and administrative body respectively are.

Stacey's distinction between the legitimate system and the shadow system within the organization corroborates the distinction by Kreps and Thornton (1984) between two forms of communication channels within the organization—the formal and the informal. Kreps and Thornton contend that there are two forms of channels in organizational communication, the formal and the informal. The informal channel of communication emerges naturally through organizational members' social interaction. The formal communication channel is prescribed by the organization's formal/organizational structure. In other words, the informal communication channel within the organization is a natural emergence; the formal communication channel within the organization is a pre-set or artificially designed establishment. Public secrets obviously are dichotomized again between the formal and informal organizational communication channels. Public secrets are usually public in the informal organizational communication channel, but secret in the formal organizational communication channel. This mismatch or discrepancy within public secrets again signals an inconsistency between the organization's formal and informal communication channels.

According to Kreps and Thornton (1984), members need relevant, reliable, and in-depth information to create effective meanings about their organizational life. The formal channels of organizational communication generally fail to provide enough information to satisfy organization members' need for meanings in their organizational life. Therefore, the informal organizational communication channels emerge to compensate for the inadequacy of formal communication channels. The relationship between the two is a negative one—the degree of prosperity of the former indicates the degree of inadequacy of the latter. Accordingly, the degree of the prosperity of public secrets, which generally travel along the informal organizational communication lines, also indicates the inadequacy of the organization's formal communication lines.

Davis (1973) also commented on the informal organization—"the organization that's not on the chart" (p. 149) as he called it. Davis believes that the grapevine is the major communication network in the informal organization. Effort to get rid of the inevitable grapevine would prove futile. A more feasible alternative is to make proactive use of the grapevine for positive benefit for the organization. Usually there are key communicators in the grapevine. Therefore, many managers attempt to get rid of the grapevine by silencing the key communicators within the grapevine. Yet Davis believes that the "grapevine is more a product of the situation than of the person" (p. 151). That is, what produces the grapevine with those "sour grapes" of rumors are not the key communicators, but the general communication climate within the organization. Consequently, silencing the key communicators that spread "rumors" along the grapevine may only produce more key communicators to take the place. Thus, the effective way to deal with the grapevine, according to Davis, is not to turn to people, but to turn to the organization.

What causes the prosperity of the grapevine, according to Davis (1973), is "information vacuum" (p. 152). The grapevine thrives paradoxically on a lack of real, relevant, and accurate information. Davis contends that when people feel reasonably secure and understand the things that matter to them, they will not find a cause to start rumors.

Taking into account the nature and characteristics of the grapevine, Davis (1973) offered several strategies to help an organization to integrate the grapevine as an ally instead of alienating it as an adversary. First, the manager should convey the facts to the key communicators. Second, managers should consult higher levels of supervision to find out what details can be made public. Third, if a decision is going to hurt some people, explain why the decision is necessary. If the decision is going to hurt only a few, inform these few first in private. Finally, "never pass the buck" (p. 154). If you cannot answer a question, do not just guess or give it a brush-off. Promise to find relevant information and keep the promise.

Echoing Kreps & Thornton, and Davis, Liu (1986) offers a diagram of Chinese communication system, categorized into the formal-institutionalized and informal-noninstitutionalized communication channels (reference may be made again to figure 1.2). Liu contends that the informal communication medium is pervasive and resistant to official suppression. Word of mouth or side-lane news, as Chinese call it, is an important form of informal-noninstitutionalized communication medium. The popular word of *rumor* often refers to such communication medium. Contrary to popular perception, Liu argues, by citing experimental evidence, that rumors are far from false. The notion that rumors are only used for emotional satisfaction regardless of objective truth is not valid. The speed at which rumors travel in free, real-life situations only prove the plausibility and logic within the rumors. People relay rumors only because they can make sense of the rumors. Experimental evidence also shows that when official information and informal information contradict each other, people more often choose to believe the latter (Liu, 1986).

Since information contained in public secrets usually travels in the informal communication channel, word of mouth is also an important medium in which public secrets spread themselves. Liu's contention, when applied to public secrets, informs that information in public secrets travels fast, enjoys accuracy, and is perceived as credible. Therefore, public secrets tend to exert great impact upon organizational members' actions and attitudes.

As I mentioned at the beginning of this section, study of the mechanism of various organizational dichotomies apparently helps our understanding of the operation of public secrets.

THE CULTURAL PHENOMENON OF TABOO

The cultural phenomenon of taboo has an interesting relevance to and can help explain the communication phenomenon of public secrets. As I discussed previously, public secrets represent an oxymoron: what is communicated in one context is kept secret or tacit in another context; what is discussable with one group of people becomes undiscussable with another group. That is, the secret side of public secrets contains a rule of "Thou-shalt-not"—"You should not talk about this here and with these people." In other words, public secrets may imply taboos that impose a rule of prohibition, advising people not to do or say certain things in certain situations.

According to Webster (1973), the word taboo comes from the Polynesian *tabu*. In ancient societies, people believed that there was a logical connection between things that bear likeness. Things bearing a likeness affect each other. For example, in Madagascar, a soldier will not eat kidneys because in Malagasy language, kidney and "shot" are the same word. Eating the delicacy of kidney can cause a soldier to be shot, as people in Madagascar reasoned. In Chinese culture, you do not give a clock as a gift, especially as a gift to an elderly person because in the language of Chinese, the pronunciation of the phrase "sending the gift of clock" is exactly the same with that of "sending someone to his/her tomb." Therefore, taboos represent an effort to avoid bad luck when people harbor certain beliefs or still lack scientific knowledge to explain the real connections among events (Webster, 1973).

Citing Charles Dickens, Browne (1984) considers taboos as "ghosts of history." Memory is where history lives. People remember doing a certain thing some time ago and then suffering a negative consequence. As a result, people stipulate rules or taboos of "thou-shalt-nots"—"You shall not do this and this, otherwise you'll suffer." As history goes on, people inherit a repository of such rules or taboos which gradually become cultural customs. When something becomes a cultural custom, people simply practice it unconsciously without further questioning the rationale behind the custom. Yet human conditions change, and the past is not always applicable to the present. Thus many taboos may become "shackles" inherited from history and haunt people like "ghosts" (Browne, 1984).

Browne (1984) also believes that taboos are relative. What is taboo in one culture may even be daily practice in another culture. What is taboo in one time may become what is espoused in another time. Using examples from real life, Browne explains how it can be a liberating experience to abolish taboos that no longer have a rationale in current conditions. At many cultural institutions (e.g., museums and parks), there is the taboo of "no touching" concerning the exhibited artifacts. One time, Browne narrated, he went to see the Liberty Bell at Independence Mall Park in Philadelphia. The tour guide invited him to touch, thump, and ring the Bell. He discovered that it was an exhilarating experience and that more happened to him than to the Bell. Thus, Browne contends, moving beyond and abolishing outmoded taboos will offer new discoveries and an enlightening experience.

The secret side of "public secrets" certainly contains taboos. Ideas from Webster and Browne may inspire us to have a better approach to taboos contained in public secrets. As explained by Webster and Browne, these taboos may be "historical ghosts," inheritance that no longer has a rationale in current reality. Abolition of taboos in public secrets may liberate people's communication and offer them an exhilarating and enlightening experience.

DEFENSIVE COMMUNICATION AND INFORMATION DISTORTION

One of the major reasons why people keep secret, in one context, their information about the workplace that they genuinely express in another context is probably that they are afraid of something; that they are defending themselves against something. A defensive communication climate is a highly possible breeder of public secrets and information distortion.

Much literature in rhetoric (e.g., Nietzsche 1990, and Burke 1990) contends that language not only reflects but also selects and deflects reality. That is, language distorts reality and what the communicators actually mean. Gibb (1961), however, contends that communication is not only a language process, but, more importantly, a people process. Fundamental improvement in communication comes from changes in interpersonal relationships. Negative interpersonal relationships can cause defensive communication climate where people communicate not for genuine expression of their minds, but for manipulation of others' perception of themselves through information distortion or camouflage. Thus we may say that defensive communication is, more accurately, anti-communication because it tries not to express and reveal but to distort and conceal.

Gibb (1961) also believes that defensive communication is reproductive, meaning that defensive communication in turn produces defensive listening. When defensive listening occurs, the message recipients become less and less able to perceive accurately the motives, the values, and the emotions of the message sender. Information or communication distortion occurs the second time in the message reception after its first occurrence in defensive message sending. Defensive communication and defensive listening mutually promote each other in the production of greater and greater information/communication distortion.

Gibb's theory of defensive communication is applicable to public secrets. Public secrets have two contexts in which they are differently manifested. In one context, they represent public, genuine information and knowledge (For the sake of ease in writing, let me call this context the public context). In another context (let me call it the secret context), they are secrets and taboos. Public secrets, in their public context, often represent normal and healthy communication. Yet, in their secret context, public secrets represent a highly defensive communication.

Values, motives, emotions, understandings, information, and knowledge that are open in the public context, now within the secret context, disappear, are camouflaged, or distorted. What is more serious, all this information disappears or distorted not so often because of unavoidable, objective restraints as because of conscientious efforts. By covering up and distorting what they genuinely share and transmit in one context, people are obviously defending or protecting themselves in another context. An effort to defend/protect oneself indicates the existence of fear. Fear, as argued by Ryan & Oestreich (1991), has much negative impact on organizational communication and health.

According to the investigation by Ryan & Oestreich (1991), fear within the organization nurtures the following problems: negative feelings about the organization (29% of survey responses), negative impact on quality or productivity (27% of the responses), negative feelings about oneself (19%), negative emotions (12%), and other negative effects (11%). Only 2% of the respondents thought fear has a positive effect. Subsumed under "negative feelings about the organization" are loss of trust or pride, increase in political or self-protective behavior, contemplated or real job transfers, and petty revenge or sabotage. Subsumed under "negative impact on quality or productivity" are lack of extra efforts, making and hiding mistakes, failure to meet deadlines and budgets, loss of effective problem solving, work on wrong priorities, poor methods, and loss of creativity, motivation, and risk taking. The total cost and loss caused by all these negative effects from fear is hard to measure, but it is surely not in the range of a small amount.

Public secrets in its secret context (where genuine information is not expressed) obviously contains information distortion and cover-up. Anthanassiades (1973) suggests a theory of insecurity-ascendancy to explain the causes of upward information distortion. The more insecure the employee feels, he argues, the more likely he/she will distort information in upward communication. The greater the employee's wish to ascend in the hierarchical ladder, the more likely the employee will distort upward information. Therefore, in an autonomous structure, employees tend to distort information less because employees feel less coerced, less defensive, and thus less inclined to perceive distortion of his/her upward communication as instrumental to attaining his/her goal. A hierarchical authority structure works the opposite way. In such a structure, employees more easily feel insecure because the hierarchical organization itself tends to breed conflict, hostility, and the like. This insecurity invites the employee to engage in more upward information distortion as a self-defensive mechanism. The hierarchical structure invites a greater wish to ascend than the autonomous structure because hierarchy itself is a pyramid of ascending ranks. A stronger wish to ascend invites a greater risk-taking spirit, which in turn engenders greater information distortion. In short, Anthanassiades' (1973) contention is that whenever an organizational climate fosters conditions of insecurity and ascendance, this climate at the same time tends to produce more upward information distortion.

Since the phenomenon of public secrets contains information distortion, I hypothesize that Anthanassiades' theory can also help explain the causes of public secrets. This hypothesis, of course, needs further investigation.

Borrowing from Weber's theoretical structure of bureaucracy and his own theory of insecurity-ascendancy to explain information distortion, Anthanassiades (1973) suggested four strategies to decrease employees' distortion of information: (1) an elaborate system of clearly-defined and interrelated rules and regulations; (2) simplification and standardization of work; (3) presence of an impersonal authority structure; and (4) promotion based on tenure and seniority. Whether these strategies can help decrease the extent of public secrets also is a matter subject to further research.

Anthanassiades' strategies directly address how to decrease upward communication distortion in the organization's official communication channel. This is rather a reactive tactic toward information/knowledge possessed by organizational members. Anthanassiades did not address the question of how to actively or proactively transform what organization members already know into public, actable knowledge. Anthanassiades' theory does not provide insight into how to achieve this proactive strategy. Also, some of Anthanassiades' suggested strategies (as mentioned previously) in order to decrease information distortion may tend to alienate employees and thus demotivate them.

Vogel (1967) provides the following reasons to explain why employees cover up information by refraining from speaking up their minds: (1) Many employees fear that expressing their true feelings about the company to their boss could be dangerous; (2) It is a fairly widespread belief that disagreeing with the boss will block promotion; (3) People are usually convinced that management is not interested in employee problems; (4) Employees often believe that they are not rewarded for good ideas; and (5) There exists a lack of supervisory accessibility and responsiveness.

Vogel (1967) suggests six strategies for building a communication climate of trust and openness, which in turn helps decrease information distortion. (1) Frankness within management. Vogel believes that if critical discussion is choked off at higher levels of the company, it ceases to flow at lower levels. (2) Supervisor accessibility. Many employees do not think managers as good listeners. One of the biggest problems that makes managers bad listeners is lack of manager accessibility. (3) Welcome for the new and different. Tolerance of all kinds of ideas will help bring out more constructive and creative ideas. (4) Visible benefits. Actual reward to good ideas is the strongest encouragement of freer expression of ideas. (5) Acceptance of criticism. Managers should regard criticism as healthy and normal, and lack of criticism as dangerous and undesirable, which is an indication that employees have given up trying to get through to management. (6) Sensitivity to employees. Employees' complaints should be carefully interpreted. A gripe about working conditions may mask a belief that the boss doesn't appreciate the individual's job performance.

Although the research of both Anthanassiades and Vogel may help explain the causes of public secrets and provide possible strategies to allay the phenomenon of public secrets, their research only addresses organizational members' informational or communicative behavior in the organization's official communication context. The connection between this context and the organization's other communication contexts is not addressed. More particularly, how does organizational members' informal, private communicative behavior compare and contrast with their public, formal communicative behavior? What insight does this comparison and contrast offer into the organization's whole communication system? Why is information covered up and/or distorted in one communicative context within the organization open and shared in another context? These questions, not addressed by Anthanassiades or Vogel, merit further investigation.

THE LEARNING ORGANIZATION

Literature on the "learning organization" has much relevance to the research of the phenomenon of public secrets which, in fundamental analysis, is an informational issue. From the literature on the "learning organization," we will realize that information-gathering and processing is the central feature of the "learning organization." This literature provides explanations of the features of the "learning organization," and the strategies that facilitate organizational learning. Understanding these features and strategies will help us better understand informational characteristics in the phenomenon of public secrets, and effective strategies that would help decrease the phenomenon of public secrets.

Chris Argyris, a Harvard professor, is one of the earliest scholars engaged in the study of "the learning organization." Initially, the argument was merely around the questions of whether there is such a thing as "the learning organization," "Do organizations learn?" "Can they learn?" Scholars knew that individuals learn, a fact that had been well established by advances in biological and psychological studies. Yet many scholars were not certain whether organizations, which possess no brain and no nerve system like what humans have, learn. Argyris and Schön (1978) argue that although the social organization does not have a physical brain and a nerve system as the human body does, it has a collective brain that is made possible by the communicative exchange between and among the brains of the individual organization members. Argyris and Schön (1978) contend that one evidence of the existence of "organizational learning" comes from such daily statements: "The management decides that…," "The company made a serious mistake and should draw a lesson from it," and "The R&D department thinks that…." If an organization learns through its collective brain which is composed of all the individual brains of its individual members, then the question may be asked about how the exchange of information among organization members as indicated in the phenomenon of public secrets contributes to or hinders organizational learning.

It was also Argyris and Schön who first introduced the concept of "double-loop" learning (Argyris & Schön, 1978). A "double-loop" learning organization, as I mentioned previously, focuses on the assumptions underlying its standards instead of merely trying to improve along a particular set of standards and dimensions. In this sense, a double-loop learning organization has a self-reflective capacity. And accordingly, "single-loop learning" should be the type that only involves the simplistic, reactive learning framework of "stimuli-response," as what animals generally engage in. Regarding the phenomenon of public secrets, the question that can be pursued here is, "Is the phenomenon of public secrets helping or hindering an organization's effort in examining the assumptions underlying its standards and prescriptions?"

The definition of "the learning organization" attempted by Aryris (1996) is, "an organization may be said to learn when it acquires information (knowledge, understanding, know-how, techniques, or practices of any kind and by whatever means)" (p. 3). Thus, to Argyris, information gathering is the defining feature of a learning organization. Argyris believes that information should be the basis for organizational action. Organizational actions not information-based are arbitrary and self-defeating.

Argyris (1996) designates the process of information-gathering in an organization as "organizational inquiry." He used inquiry not in the colloquial sense of scientific or juridical investigation but in a more fundamental sense which originates from the work of John Dewey (1938): an intertwining of thought and action that proceeds from doubt to the resolution of doubt. In this Deweyan inquiry, doubt is interpreted as the experience of a "problematic situation," triggered by the mismatch between the desired result from an action and the actual result from this action. To make it simpler, inquiry is an attempt to solve a problem by decreasing doubt. Does the phenomenon of public secrets help to decrease or increase doubt within the organization? Thus, does this phenomenon encourage or discourage inquiry?

Weick's model of equivocality goes well with Argyris' (1996) concept of inquiry. According to Weick (1969), the purpose of organization is cooperation with others so that the cooperative network therein will provide the organization with enough and detailed information to interpret complex problems and develop meaningful strategies to deal with those problems. For successful organizational actions, there should be a balance between the equivocality of the situation and the equivocality of the needed information. In other words, the more complex the situation, the more information is needed. The process, as defined by Weick (1969), of gathering enough information to match with every existent component of the situational complexity, is exactly the same with Argyris' (1996) concept of inquiry. In terms of essential features of the learning organization, Weick provides us with a cooperative network, which, in turn, furnishes the necessary informational equivocality for successful organizational actions. Once again, the question inspired for this research is, "Is 'public secrets' helping or hindering the cooperative network within an organization?"

The cooperativeness in Weick's "cooperative network" is echoed back by Argyris. Argyris (1996) believes that an organization is not a collection of separate individuals, but a collectivity of interdependent and interlocked individuals (pp. 6–8). Interdependence between and among organization members distinguishes an organization from a mob. Every individual surely possesses various information and knowledge, much of which is contributive to the solution(s) of organizational problems if these individuals do form their organization with a collective goal. Yet in a mob, because of a lack of a systemic interdependence and networking between and among the individuals, information and "knowledge held by individuals fails to enter into the stream of distinctively organizational thought and action, organizations know *less* than their members" (Argyris, 1996, p. 6). In an organization, on the other hand, the information system, which is very much like the nerve system of a living body, enables the organization members to fluidly exchange information throughout the organization. This fluid exchange of information helps to assure that organizational actions are information-based. Once again, the question inspired here for this research is, "Do public secrets make an organization more like a mob or a real organization?"

Interdependence, as another essential feature of a learning organization, is further researched and described by other scholars of the learning organization. W. Edwards Deming was a prominent one among them. In both of his most famous books, Out of Crisis (1986) and The New Economics (1993), Deming talks about the distinction between a learning organization and a non-learning one, although he does not explicitly use the term of "the learning organization." Deming deals with this distinction by introducing two cycles of actions, the old cycle and the new cycle. In the old cycle of organizational action (please refer to figure 2.2, which is not exactly a cycle though), a product is first designed, although we are not clear about the yardstick on which the design is based. Second, the designed product is produced. How many and how good the products should be, we do not know. Finally, the producer tries to sell this product.

Design a product ——▶ Produce the product ——▶ Try to sell the product

Figure 2.2 The Old Cycle of Organizational Action

In this old cycle of organizational action, we do not see any interdependence. At most, we see dependence. The third step depends on the second step. The second step depends on the first step. This one-directional dependence engenders an obvious high risk. If the design happens to be bad, everything else will by no means fare well. No feedback is found in this old cycle of production.

In Deming's new cycle (which is truly a cycle, please refer to figure 2.3) of organizational action, we do see an interdependence. Plan influences action. Results of the action are studied. Depending on the lesson drawn from the study, decision is made about how to revise the action. The revised action will feed new elements into another cycle of planning. This new cycle of organizational action, unlike the old one, is not a one-time, one-directional, and self-dependent action. It is a flowing, non-stop, interactive, and balanced process, a reflection of the very image of the living life. Deming's systemic cycle of organizational action represents a constant processing of information, which finds a supportive voice in Argyris' concept of "information gathering." The question that Deming may lead us to think in terms of this research is, "Is 'public secrets' promoting the old cycle of organizational action or the new cycle?"

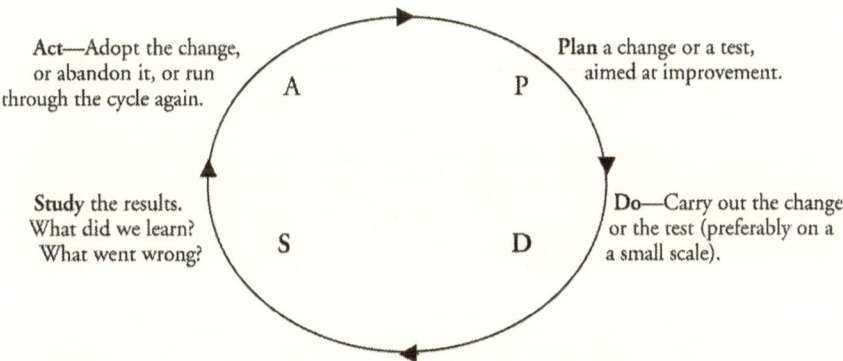

Figure 2.3 Deming's New Cycle of Organizational Action or the P D S A Cycle
(From page 135 of Deming's *The New Economics*)

Echoing Deming's new cycle of organizational action, Cohen (1997) developed the cycle of "intellectual capital" (please refer to figure 2.4). Unlike Deming's cycle, Cohen's cycle has a new element in it, the collaborative infrastructure. This infrastructure is an information storage and retrieval system. It contains all the knowledge and information that comes from the circular process of deciding, acting, interpreting & learning, and applying knowledge. Cohen calls the information contained in this infrastructure "intellectual capital." He defines intellectual capital as "content plus action." Intellectual content—patents, proposals, or the knowledge in people's heads—has no economic value until it is embodied in action. It is the products based on the ideas that generate revenue, not the ideas or the patents themselves. Thus, Cohen seems not only to emphasize the importance of information gathering for a learning organization, but attaches more importance to information storage, retrieving, and, above all, application. What are the implications of the phenomenon of public secrets upon "intellectual capital?" One thing is clear. Since information in public secrets is only sharable, but not actable, public secrets do not contribute to an organization's "intellectual capital."

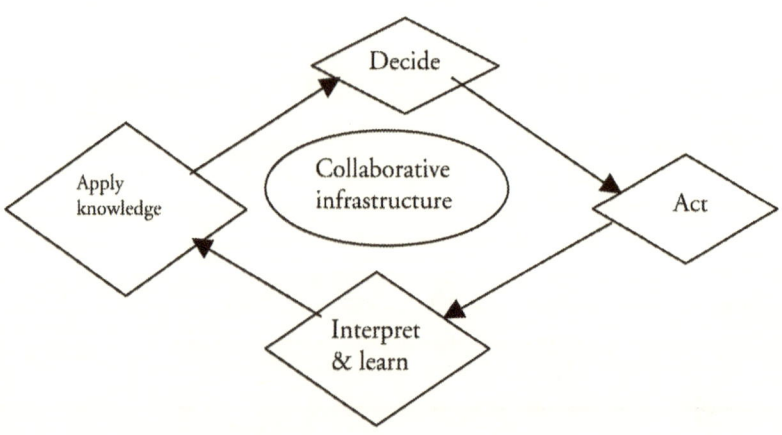

Figure 2.4 Cohen's Cycle of Intellectual Capital

Peter Senge is another enthusiastic advocate of the learning organization. In his influential book, <u>The fifth discipline: The art and practice of the learning organization</u> (1990), he offers five "disciplines" that builds a learning organization. These five disciplines are: (1) systems thinking, (2) personal mastery, (3) mental models; (4) building shared vision; and (5) team learning.

Systems thinking signifies universal principles and purpose that govern every single and imaginable component within an organization, be it as small as a family or as big as a nation. At the same time, all the components of the system enjoy their own contributive and autonomous uniqueness. On one hand, there is much dependence in terms of the organizational purpose. Every component depends on this purpose as its Northern Star for actions. On the other hand, there is much independence within every individual element. This combination of dependence and independence is interdependence, which runs as a common thread in the fabric of the learning organization. This interdependence blesses the organization with a homeostatic dynamism, a co-existence of stability and growth.

By "personal mastery," Senge (1990) refers to the capacity to clarify what is most important to oneself and the ability to achieve it. In a learning organization, people do not fear their individual, inner consciousness. Rather, they find this consciousness as the root of energy for the realization of the collective, organizational goal. A learning organization endeavors to decrease personal confusion by striving for congruence between individual aspirations and organizational ideals.

By "mental models," Senge (1990) means the capacity to reflect on our internal pictures of the world to see how they shape our thinking and actions. Senge believes that lucid understanding of mental models or underlying assumptions is the most effective method to solve conflicts, many of which occur not because of inherent differences, but because of confused perceptions of reality, biased by clouded mental models. In terms of mental models, Senge obviously draws heavily from the work of Chris Argyris, especially the latter's work on "doubleloop" learning.

"Building shared visions" is connected with the systemic viewpoint of the learning organization. Shared visioning is the ability of an organization to create a deeply meaningful and broadly-held common sense of direction. Too often, visions are leader-designed instead of organizationally constructed. As a result, they may be visions, but not shared. The safe order of shared visions comes from the perilous but necessary chaos of free-flowing voices and information (reference may be made to Stacey's "innovative space" mentioned previously). Many leaders and managers do not understand this point, as Senge (1990) contends. They believe that order and structure come from control and regimentation, which actually produce stagnation. And stagnation and order are too often mistakenly equalized. For the vision to be shared, the individual sharer must perceive that he/she plays an active role and has an imbedded interest in the proper cultivation and formulation of that vision.

By "team learning," Senge refers to the capacity for collective intelligence and productive conversation. This concept is obviously connected with the previous concept of "building shared visions." "Team learning" is actually the process whereby team members build shared visions. "Team" indicates "integration," "collectivity," "converging," and "dialogue," instead of "disintegration," "isolation," "egocentrism," and "monologue." The "learning" part comes from an individualistic individual; the "team" part comes from a "collectivistic" individual. The integration of the two sides can only become possible through respect and trust for the team, which, in turn, is a reward from respect and trust of the individual.

The first discipline of Senge's learning organization is the capstone of the architecture of such an organization. The rest of the other four disciplines are the building blocks of the edifice of the learning organization. They are obviously different manifestations of the systems thinking in various aspects of an organization.

Under the inspiration of Senge, the question that may be asked for this research can be, "Does the phenomenon of 'public secrets' contribute to or hinder the five disciplines of the learning organization?"

Nonaka & Takeuchi go a step further than many scholars in their research of the learning organization. Argyris, Weick, Deming, Senge, and many others perceive the process of information gathering as a major feature of the learning organization. Nonaka & Takeuchi (1995) believe that mere information gathering falls short of the learning organization in its real sense. A real learning organization not only gathers information, but, more importantly, creates knowledge. Knowledge is a broader concept than information. Information is usually mechanistic, standardized, impoverished, and manipulated for easy electronic transaction. Knowledge, which includes information, can also be intuitive, subjective, subtle, unexpressed, and yet highly valuable if properly tapped. According to Nonaka & Takeuchi (1995), there are two types of knowledge that helps an organization to learn, the tacit knowledge and the explicit knowledge. An organization learns through knowledge creation, which, in turn, comes from an interactive conversion between the tacit knowledge and the explicit knowledge.

The tacit knowledge is usually possessed by individual organization members. This type of knowledge is tacit because it is not easily visible and expressible. Tacit knowledge includes individuals' private beliefs, understandings, unexpressed information, subtle techniques accumulated through long experience, general feelings, and rough concepts. Explicit knowledge, on the other hand, can easily be processed and transmitted, electronically or otherwise. Explicit knowledge is usually systematically recorded in organizational documents, regulations, agendas, pamphlets and the like, making this type of knowledge easily retrievable. "But the subjective and intuitive nature of tacit knowledge makes it difficult to process or transmit the acquired knowledge in any systemic and logical manner" (Nonaka & Takeuchi, 1995, p. 9). And Nonaka and Takeuchi, in the same book, also contend that the bulk of the knowledge that an organization can hope to possess exists in the form of tacit knowledge.

Nonaka & Takeuchi (1995) support the view that a learning organization is a living organism, not merely an information processing machine. Within this context, "sharing an understanding of what the company stands for, where it is going, what kind of a world it wants to live in, and how to make that world a reality becomes much more crucial than processing objective information" (Nonaka & Takeuchi, 1995, p. 9).

Nonaka & Takeuchi (1995) provide four modes of knowledge creation: from tacit to tacit, from tacit to explicit, from explicit to tacit, and from explicit to explicit (please refer to figure 2.5 that follows).

	Tacit knowledge	*To*	Explicit knowledge
Tacit Knowledge	Socialization		Externalization
From			
Explicit Knowledge	Internalization		Combination

Figure 2.5 Knowledge Conversion Modes

In the socialization or tacit to tacit mode of knowledge creation, organization members interact/socialize informally and exchange what they know in a spontaneous way. What happens in Honda is one example of this type of knowledge creation. Honda has "brainstorming camps" where employees can have tea and meals together. In this informal context, people exchange spontaneously what they know about their own specialized area, their understanding of some organizational problems, their conceived solutions to some of the problems, and the like. "There is one understood taboo in such socialization: criticism without constructive suggestions" (Nonaka & Takeuchi, 1995, p. 63).

The externalization mode of knowledge creation, according to Nonaka & Takeuchi (1995), "is typically seen in the process of concept creation and is triggered by dialogue or collective reflection" (p. 64). The use of metaphors, analogies, concepts, hypotheses, or models can help transform tacit knowledge into explicit knowledge.

In the internalization mode of knowledge creation, individual organization members internalize the publicly available knowledge through personal actions and experience. Similarities among such actions and experience by different individuals will help to form shared mental models (reference may be made to previous discussion of Senge's "mental models") and technical know-how.

"Combination is a process of systemizing concepts into a knowledge system" (Nonaka & Takeuchi, 1995, p. 67). This mode of knowledge creation involves exchanging, sorting, adding, combining, and categorizing between and among different bodies of explicit knowledge. Channels used for this mode of knowledge creation include documents, meetings, telephone conversations, or computer communication network.

The question that Nonaka & Takeuchi inspire for this research is, "How does the phenomenon of 'public secrets' fit with the four modes of knowledge creation?" As I explained previously, public secrets contain sharable knowledge that fails to become actable knowledge. Sharable knowledge in the secret context of public secrets may be more properly called implicit knowledge, that is, knowledge understood but not expressed. To make Nonaka & Takeuchi's table of knowledge creation more complete, implicit knowledge may be added to tacit knowledge and explicit knowledge as the third type of knowledge. Thus I suggest a revised table of knowledge creation as follows (please refer to figure 2.6 on next page).

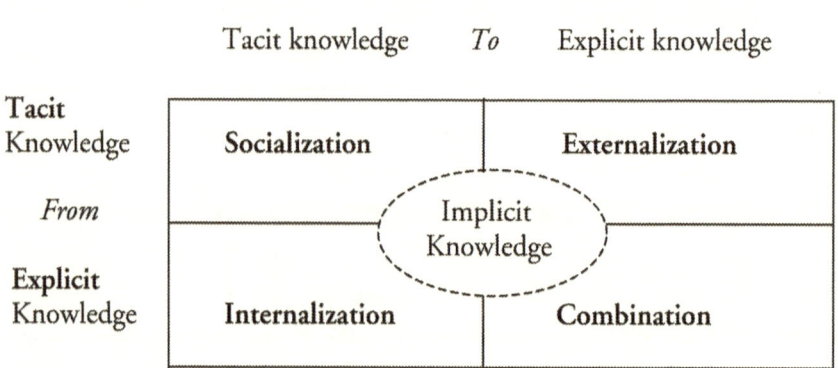

Figure 2.6 Revised Table of Knowledge Conversion Modes

The dotted oval around "implicit knowledge" signifies that the boundary between implicit knowledge and other modes of knowledge creation is porous. That is, there is a mutual influence between the two. Implicit knowledge is rather an intermediate step between tacit knowledge and explicit knowledge. Tacit knowledge, according to Nonaka and Takeuchi (1995), is still unexpressed and lies latent within the individual. Explicit knowledge is fully expressed and is accessible to general organization members. Implicit knowledge is in between, expressed in one context (the public side) and unexpressed in the other context (the secret side). Implicit knowledge (as may be manifested in public secrets) is rather like a bridge between tacit knowledge and explicit knowledge, signifying organizational members' effort to transform their individual tacit knowledge into public, explicit knowledge. Unfortunately, implicit knowledge in public secrets is not usually perceived in the positive image of a bridge by administrators.

More recent researchers on the learning organization, instead of mainly studying the major conceptual components or the essential features of the learning organization, are giving more attention to the *how* rather than the *why* and *what* of a learning organization. That is, they are trying to find the methods, facilities, and strategies to create the essential features of the learning organization.

Schein (1993) discussed how to start and maintain dialogue, one facility of interaction that contributes to organizational learning. Schein believes that the facilitator of dialogue/discussion groups plays an important role in starting and maintaining dialogue. The facilitator can engage in the following activities: (1) organize the physical space so that it is as nearly a circle as possible; (2) introduce the general concept and ask members to recall relevant experience; (3) ask people to share their experience with their neighbor; (4) ask the member to share with the group the experience; (5) ask the group to reflect on the experiences by having each person in turn talk about his/her reactions; (6) allow conversations flow naturally; (7) intervene for necessary clarification; and (8) close the session by inviting any comments.

Issacs (1993) introduced a chart (please refer to figure 2.7 on the following page) which contains helpful concepts to facilitate conversation. *Deliberation* of one's own ideas is needed when there is disagreement and lack of understanding. Deliberation is also needed when the member makes his/her personal evaluation of options and strategies. When conversation develops, there will inevitably emerge disagreement, disconfirmation, challenge, or attack. At such heated moments, the member needs to *suspend* her ideas, and engage in internal listening to be more receptive to differences and more conducive to building mutual trust. *Discussion* usually involves advocating of one's ideas, competing for validity for one's ideas, and convincing others of one's ideas. Discussion is an active or even aggressive form of conversation, according to Isaacs. *Dialogue* involves frank confrontation of one's own and others' assumptions, revelation of feelings, and building of common ground. *Dialectic* means the exploration of the opposite side of everything or discovery of oppositions. *Metalogue* is a high form of dialogue, engendering the convergence of feelings and thinking within the group. Metalogue helps build new shared assumptions and culture. *Debate* is resolving of conflicts through the battle of logic and "beating down." All these concepts can help either to start or maintain the flow of conversation, which, in turn, facilitates the creation of knowledge, the essential feature of the learning organization as contended by Nonaka & Takeuchi (1995).

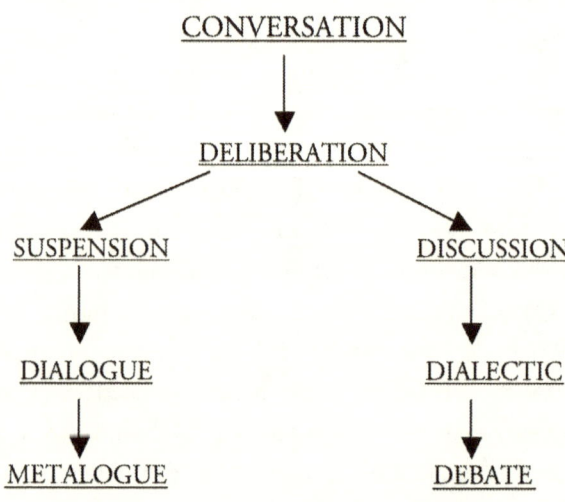

Figure 2.7 Ways of Talking Together

Quality circles are another way to increase conversation, dialogue, and thus discovery of ideas within an organization. Quality circles are composed of organization members from all levels of the organization who meet regularly to discuss and try to solve job-related problems (Dewar, 1980). The concept of quality circles, though sharing similarity with Nonaka & Takeuchi's (1995) socialization mode of knowledge creation, offers us another strategy to involve organization members in the discovery of possible solutions to organizational problems.

All the strategies Schein, Issacs, and Dewar offer increase learning, communication, and congruence among various components of an organization and thus these strategies promise to decrease the phenomenon of "public secrets."

COMMUNICATION, MOTIVATION, AND ORGANIZATIONAL HEALTH

By introducing literature on the relationship among communication, motivation, and organizational health, this section intends to direct attention toward the relationship among public secrets (a communicational phenomenon in nature), motivation, and organizational health. Much literature has demonstrated that organization members' role in participation and organizational communication impacts their motivation and organizational health.

Timbers (1966) contends that people are moved by two things: the carrot or the stick. In other words, people are either moved by a satisfaction of their wishes, or by fear. Timbers believes that in this age of industry and democracy, fear as a great mover of people has lost its potency. Consequently, managers can only hope to motivate employees by an effort to meet their wishes wherein the major instrument is communication which, in turn, is composed of listening, understanding, and cooperating.

According to Timbers (1966), people have a basic need for a feeling of belonging. Thus, employees need to know what is going within their workplace; they need to have the ears of the manager about their wishes, worries, and ideas. Timbers espouses consultative management. The question, "What do you think?", is not a casual greeting. It is a display of respect and care, saying, "You are one of us. What you think and feel matters." Also, the simple question, "What do you think?", frequently opens the floodgate to a flow of valuable ideas that are contributive to the general effectiveness of the organization.

More importantly, Timbers believes that consultative management enables employees to be more receptive to organizational plans and initiatives. Organizational policies, strategies, initiatives, and the like, if formulated with adequate participation from employees, are perceived by these employees not cynically as "their ideas," but sincerely as "our ideas." This positive perception frequently plays a decisive role in leading organizational initiatives either into success or into failure. Resistance to change, O'Toole (1996) eloquently argues, is the major enemy to effective leadership. A genuine leader is able to lead change that is followed and practiced with willingness.

To bring about effective communication and thus employee motivation into an organization, Timbers (1966) explains the communicative barrier and several strategies to overcome this barrier. Status and position or an assumption of them, Timbers contends, are a formidable barrier to genuine communication. Several strategies may be effective in overcoming this barrier. First, Timbers espouses face-to-face communication throughout the organization as the most efficient and economical strategy. Second, top management should take sincere and concrete actions to establish a free and permissive climate favoring upward communication. Third, a people-centered rather than a production-centered attitude by management along with an open door in fact as well as in word are other essential elements for effective organizational communication.

Taking Timbers' contentions in consideration, we can understand the impact of public secrets upon employee motivation by understanding the impact of public secrets upon or the relationship of public secrets with an organization's communication climate. The strategies Timbers suggested may also prove helpful in abating possible negative impact from the phenomenon of "public secrets."

Lori Sefton (1999) conducted a quantitative study of Plant and Service Operations (PSO), a service organization on the campus of Southern Illinois University at Carbondale (SIUC). Results of her study show that employee participation is positively related to job satisfaction, communication satisfaction, and organizational commitment. The study reflects a participation index mean of 2.85 on a five-point scale. The job satisfaction index mean, the communication satisfaction index mean, and the organizational commitment mean were respectively 3.85, 3.32, and 3.58, all above the mid-point on each index. Sefton (1999) claims that employee participation should largely be manifested in their participation in information sharing and decision-making. This is understandable because, in our age of information, participation is, more than ever before, mental rather than manual. That is, organization members affect their organization through their mental power rather than their physical force. The flow and use of information in decision making acquires unprecedented importance in terms of participation.

According to Maslow (1954), humans have different levels of needs. The lowest level need is life or survival (food, water, warmth, etc.), the second level need is security (shelter, safety, etc.), the third level need is belongingness or affiliation (group membership, affection, etc.), the fourth level need is respect or esteem (honor, recognition, etc.), and the highest level need is self-actualization (fulfilling personal potential). The need for self-actualization is probably the most difficult, and thus the most scarce, the most precious, and the most dreamed of. It is obvious that one cannot reach self-actualization without adequate use of what is genuinely in one's mind for contribution to the group. It is inconceivable to claim that organization members are self-actualized without being able to use their knowledge, understandings, feelings, and aspirations in the organization's process of decision-making.

In conformity with Maslow's theory, Herzberg (1973) claims that motivation is based on two kinds of needs: hygiene needs and motivational needs. The former echoes the lower level needs in Maslow's hierarchy of human needs, including extrinsic rewards such as salary, external recognition, and social status. Motivational needs echo Maslow's higher level needs, including intrinsic rewards such as personal fulfillment and enjoyment of work. According to Herzberg

(1973), once employees' hygiene needs are satisfied, motivation comes from satisfaction of the motivational needs. Again, it would be inconceivable how an organization is able to meet its members' motivational needs without enabling them to utilize their mental resources in helping to decide where the organization is going and should go.

McGregor (1960) contends that the best method to motivate people is to facilitate conditions that allow people to realize their own goals in their striving for the organizational goals. This method can only be made possible by open communication in all possible directions, shared decision making, respect, and compassion.

Barnard (1938) argues that three things make an organization possible: communication, cooperation, and common purpose. He further contends that communication is the key to the realization of the other two elements. Individual motivation, according to Barnard, is conducive to viable and genuine communication within an organization. Individual motivation, in turn, is enhanced and protected by the informal framework of interactions in the organization which affect beliefs, values, customs, habits, and other cultural elements of the organization. For the research of public secrets, Barnard's theory implies that it is important to study communication that occurs in the informal framework of an organization because this communication impacts organization members' individual motivation.

According to Gibb (1961), whose other contentions I introduced previously, there are two kinds of communication climates in the organization: supportiveness and defensiveness. The former enhances frankness, problem solution, and spontaneity. The latter breeds distrust, easy offense, and information distortion. The former focuses on individual growth, integration, and reality which in turn lead to high productivity. The latter focuses on depersonalization, control, power, status, and rules which in turn lead to low productivity. Gibb's theory can help determine whether public secrets is contributive or detrimental to organizational health by determining whether public secrets go together with supportiveness or defensiveness.

To help create an organizational communication climate of supportiveness, Gibb (1978) introduces his TORI theory. TORI stands for four concepts respectively: trust (trusting oneself and others), opening (self-disclosing and opening up of communication channels), realizing (fulfillment of individual potential), and interdependence (cooperation and community). The key element in the TORI theory, Gibb contends, is the "T" or trust which simplifies, integrates, and unites. This contention of Gibb's supports that of Kouzes and Posner (1993) who believe that credibility is the core of effective leadership. Gibb's TORI theory is helpful in discovery of strategies to decrease the phenomenon of public secrets if they proves detrimental to organizational health.

Follett (1940) wrote about three methods for dealing with organizational problems: domination, compromise, and integration. Domination basically claims, "Shut up and do what I tell you." Compromise says, "You have to sacrifice your small interests for the sake of the big interests." Integration says, "Don't worry. We can arrive at a strategy that utilizes everyone's aspirations and knowledge." Follett gives most support to the integration style. According to this style, organizational "orders" are not prescribed, but emerge naturally out of organizational reality that is informed by organization members' knowledge of this reality. Such orders are willingly followed because they are not a dictatorial imposition but an understanding reflection of common wishes and knowledge (Follett, 1971). With the inspiration by Follett, we may ask this question for the research of public secrets: "Is the phenomenon of 'public secrets' a manifestation of the integration style in solving organizational conflicts?"

Likert (1961) proposed four different management styles: the exploitative-authoritative style, the benevolent-authoritative style, the consultative style, and the participative style. Simply put, the first style says, "You are here to work for me and listen to my orders." The second style says, "You are here to work for us and listen to my orders." The third style says, "I'd like to give a listening to your opinion to make my decision." The fourth style says, "I need to utilize your ideas to make our decision." Likert espouses the last style. Genuine communication is the basis for this style. Likert believes that, for the purpose of genuine communication, ideas, opinions, knowledge, and feedback from organization members need to be incorporated into organizational planning. The participative style of management is characterized by a congruence between informal and formal communications within the organization. Thus public secrets do not seem to go together with the participative management style.

THEORETICAL RATIONALE FOR RESEARCH QUESTIONS

From what I can extract from existing relevant literature, I am able to draw the following conclusions: (1) There exists different communication channels within the organization, roughly divided into the formal and the informal; (2) These two communication channels possess different features and are not always congruent with each other; (3) The communication phenomenon of public secrets is theoretically possible and empirically understandable; that is, organization members may cover up, in one communication channel, what they genuinely express in another communication channel in the organizational context; (4) A defensive organizational communication climate has a negative impact upon organizational health, by causing, for example, fear and information and communication distortion; (5) The phenomenon of public secrets may signal a dysfunctional communication system within an organization and is probably against the concept of the learning organization; and (6) How organization members communicate impacts their motivation and the organization's health.

Yet many questions remain unanswered. If there exists a discrepancy between organizational members' private, informal communication and their formal, institutionalized communication, how does this discrepancy exist and operate? To what extent does it exist? Why does it exist? How exactly does this discrepancy impact organizational health and organizational members' quality of work? Is this impact measurable? To what extent is it measurable? How can we decrease its possible negative impact on organizational health?

More specifically, the present project explores the following research questions:

RQ1: Does the communication phenomenon of public secrets exist, and, if yes, how widespread is this phenomenon?

RQ2: What factors do respondents perceive as contributing to the emergence of public secrets?

RQ3: What do respondents perceive as the impact of public secrets on organizational health and organizational members' quality of work?

RQ4: In what areas do public secrets exist?

RQ5: Are the suggested strategies to allay the phenomenon of public secrets effective in respondents' perception?

To search for answers to these research questions, I employed a triangulated research method that involves case illustrations, surveys, and interviews. Rationale for this research method is offered in Chapter Three.

3
METHODS

This chapter addresses the following issues: adoption of triangulated research methods, conceptual context for the study, selection of the subject population, design of the survey instrument, use of Web technology, survey procedures and outcomes, and interview procedures and outcomes.

ADOPTION OF TRIANGULATED RESEARCH METHODS

Symon and Cassel (1998) argue that there is no best research method; there is only the best research method for a specific research question in a specific research context. To abstractly and indiscriminately argue that a certain research method is the best or better than others or is the only scientific method is not reasonable or fair. If I want to study the private life of a famous writer, for example, I probably should read this writer's diaries, interview his/her family and personal friends, and visit the place where he/she lives or lived. On the other hand, if I want to know how many customers in every one hundred such as a certain product and why, I probably should construct a survey instrument to solicit responses from a representative sample of the involved customers. Thus, different research questions require different research methods that possess different strengths and deficiencies. Frequently, the best method for a research project, especially one involving different types of research questions, is a combination of several research methods (Symon & Cassel, 1998).

The present study involves investigation of a possible communication phenomenon, whether this phenomenon exists, how widespread the phenomenon exists, how it exists, what are the causes of, consequences from, and strategies to alleviate this phenomenon. Thus, in rough configuration, this study necessitates three types of tasks: understanding of a phenomenon, investigation of the scope of existence of the phenomenon, and solicitation of respondents' perception concerning the operation of the phenomenon. Correspondingly, case illustrations are provided to facilitate the understanding of the phenomenon, the survey method is used to investigate the scope of existence of the phenomenon and solicit respondents' perception, and interviews are used to further solicit respondents' ideas and to validate survey process and results. Yet in actuality, of course, these three methods cannot be employed with such clear-cut divisions. Overlap is both inevitable and desirable in the sense that different research methods complement each other's strengths and compensate for each other's deficiencies. What follows is a further explanation of the rationale for the Triangulated research methods.

First, as already can be seen in the section "Illustrations of 'Public Secrets'" in Chapter One, I extracted, from literature, some illustrative cases that help provide a better empirical understanding of the communication phenomenon of public secrets. Research through case literature is an approach that possesses historical validity. History enjoys a temporal scope and longitudinal validity that is largely absent in horizontal studies (such as a survey of a current sampling) which only promise well in spatial (but not chronological) representativeness and validity. Cases in particular are historical records for a research topic. Case descriptions are rich in detail and thus promise better totality and comprehensiveness in representing the research target. Working from cases that come from actual reality can also help the researcher avoid falling into abstract, logical extrapolations that may not help applicability to the concrete, multifaceted reality.

As apparent from a reading of the case illustrations in Chapter One, the literature from which the cases come is broader than is the general academic understanding of literature. The selected cases involve Chinese history, the governmental agency of NASA, U.S. business, and even a fable. By including a variety of case types, I intend to illustrate the ubiquity of the communication phenomenon of public secrets, and to show that this phenomenon exists not only in the present, but also in history. It exists not only in one culture, but also in other cultures. It exists not only in academic literature, but also in "non-academic" literature such as a fable. As reflection of reality, academic literature is generally direct, scientific, prescribed by stringent academic stipulations, and thus may be mechanistic and impoverished as it may only reflect the manifested/surfaced reality that is observable or measurable to the researcher. Nonacademic literature (e.g., memoirs, fables and even legends), though generally literary and even surrealistic, can be a more condensed and comprehensive reflection of the experienced reality. Nonacademic literature, more often than not, is written by *participants* and insiders of a certain reality. Academic literature frequently is written by *observers* of a certain reality (Symon & Cassell, 1998). Scientific observation may often involve intrusive intervention which in turn may engender bias. This fact may also off some strength to nonacademic literature over academic literature in terms of validity. Furthermore, academic efforts usually have a more immediate purpose for publication than nonacademic efforts, inducing the former to incur narrower selection and consequently deflection of data, manipulation for inner logical coherence, and a restrained investment in time and energy. With all these considerations, I included, in this academic study, "nonacademic" literature in my illustration of the communication phenomenon of "public secrets."

Second, I used interviews (please refer to Appendix D for the interview protocol) as a channel for data collection. Interviews enjoy one advantage over surveys: richness and depth of data. Although surveys possess good inclusiveness and representativeness in terms of horizontal scope, surveys do not have very good inclusiveness and exhaustiveness in terms of response variety and depth. The number of answer choices in any survey instrument is limited. This limited number can easily exclude possible and even important operant variables from the instrument. The option of the "*other*" entry after the given answer choices actually does not solve the problem well. Usually too few participants in a survey actually choose to write opinions into the survey. Checking boxes may be perceived as the only "legitimate" task required by a survey (Babbie, 1990).

Interviews, on the other hand, can help compensate for this deficiency of surveys. Interviews are less intrusive in the sense that they do not "put words into the mouths" of the study participants. Surveys ask people to choose from what is already given. Interviews ask people to give what *they* have. Because of this, interviews may serve as a good "reconnaissance" for the design of the survey instrument and validation of the survey results. Solicited opinions from some initial interviewees will help make answer choices in a survey instrument less arbitrary and biased. Since survey results may be biased because of the restraint from standardized answer choices, interviews may also serve as a check and validation of survey results. In the case of this study, interviews were done both before the design of the survey instrument as "reconnaissance" and after the administration of the survey as validation.

Although focus groups were originally planned for the study, they failed to materialize because of repeated difficulty in scheduling and, more importantly, because of participants' greater willingness for interviews. Further explanation is offered later on in this chapter as to why interviews were a viable replacement of focus groups. Despite the fact that no focus group was done, it may be necessary to mention one practical problem that future researchers need to be cautious about in case of focus groups. Since the study of public secrets involves exploration of the private/informal side of organization members' communication about their workplace, it should be assured that the formal/organizational communication context (often incompatible with the private/informal communication) does not emerge in a specific focus group session. That is, when people from the same workplace are involved in one focus group, they may not, because of a certain configuration of members of various ranks and from various departments, express the informal/private side of their communication about their workplace. Thus the interviewer fails to solicit the participants' informal or private opinions about their organization. To study public secrets or things that people do not usually talk about in public/formal/institutionalized contexts does pose a practical difficulty upon the researcher. Such research somewhat smacks of spy work.

Despite numerous advantages, interviews and focus groups of a considerable number may be too demanding upon the researcher in terms of time investment, and thus negatively impact the scope of the study. To strike a balance between scope and availability of time, between depth and comprehensiveness of data, I also used surveys as another channel for data collection (please refer to Appendix A for the survey instrument).

Survey is an efficient and comparatively economical method to acquire data with horizontal scope and representativeness, although survey can cause error variance because of its attempt to frame all individual participants into one standardized questionnaire. Survey is the best way to determine how widespread a current phenomenon is among a specific or general population (Babbie, 1990). Because this research involves study of the extent to which the phenomenon of public secrets exists, the survey method is appropriate. Public secrets represent a phenomenon in organizational communication which necessarily involves groups of people rather than separate individuals. The more extensive scope facilitated by the survey method is appropriate for study of an organizational phenomenon.

CONCEPTUAL CONTEXT OF STUDY

The phenomenon of public secrets may exist in various contexts. For example, secrets in the family may become expressed and shared information with strangers on a plane. The vice versa may also be true. Secrets in peaceful time may become shared knowledge in war or in time of other disasters such as an earthquake. The vice versa may also be true. What is considered as taboo and secret in one culture may be shared as daily practice in another culture. More specifically in the organizational setting, public secrets may exist in the following forms: (1) Public knowledge among general organization members is kept secret and tacit when it comes to managers and administrators; (2) Knowledge shared in informal settings (e.g., in the hallway, at off-work time and locations) is kept secret and tacit in formal settings (e.g., organizational meetings and documents); (3) Public knowledge among managers and administrators is kept secret and tacit for general organizational members; and (4) Public knowledge shared among one group of organizational members is kept secret and tacit among another group. This study focuses on public secrets that exist in the first two forms with an emphasis on the possible dichotomy between general organizational members and the informal organizational communication channel on one hand, and managers, administrators, and the formal organizational communication channel on the other hand.

The conceptual context, or more accurately, the target, of my research project is the *work*place where people generally spend the majority of their waking hours. In the workplaces of some professions, people may not work the typical schedule of eight hours a day, five days a week. Yet no matter what kind of schedule is adopted, the workplace is where people spend time and energy either preparing for future livelihood (e.g., schools where students prepare for their future jobs) or earning for actual, present livelihood. In the workplace, people expend themselves, first of all, for the extrinsic motivation of compensation that is generally in the form of a salary. In the case of internships, people may work for the required experience for their future salaried jobs.

The workplace is different from the "life place" where people expend themselves generally for the intrinsic motivation of friendship, fun, hobbies, or personal goals. "Life places" may include family, recreational center, fishing site, party, church, or travel locations. Compared with the workplace, the life place is more loose and spontaneous, less organized and governed.

The traditional workplace, however, has several conspicuous characteristics. First, there is a structural hierarchy in the workplace usually with an uneven distribution of power. Second, people work for a paid salary in the workplace. Third, prescribed positions and clear job descriptions dictate that everyone usually works in his or her own "box." Based on these characteristics of the workplace, this study did not involve, for example, self-employed people or people engaging in home-based business.

The conceptual framework of my study, though targeting one type of communication phenomenon, may involve a variety of workplaces that include volunteer organizations, service industry, manufacturing industry, education, health care, and government. Life places such as those mentioned in the previous paragraph did not receive major attention in my study. However, my study does involve people's talk, in their life places, about their workplaces. To be more exact, communication in and about the workplace is my specific research target. Communication about the workplace, of course, can also happen in life places. Therefore, to straighten up the confusion here, I would say that my *research target* is the workplace; that is, through my research, I intend to achieve a better understanding of one communication phenomenon in the workplace. Yet *data location* or *resources* for my research may go beyond the workplace into the life place. That is, data for my study of public secrets, though a phenomenon in the workplace, come not only from the organization members' communication within their workplace and during their work time, but may also come from the members when they are not in their workplace and/or not during their work time. However, I did not seek non-organizational members' talk about the workplace because my study intends to compare and contrast between organizational members', not non-organizational members', informal and formal communications.

SELECTION OF THE SUBJECT POPULATION

To operationalize the study, I identified a large public research institution in the Midwest as the subject organization for my study.[1] This institution meets the major characteristics of the traditional workplace as previously explained in this chapter. First, the institution has a structural hierarchy with administrative ranks ranging from the department chair to the President, and with academic ranks ranging from Instructor to Professor. Second, people employed with the institution work for a paid salary. Third, prescribed positions and clear job descriptions dictate that everyone employed with the institution has his/her own role and responsibility.

For better uniformity within the subject population, I only selected faculty of the subject institution, both tenured and untenured. Administrators, instructors, retired faculty, students, and those who have severed their affiliation with the institution were not included in the study. All available e-mail addresses (a total of 937) of faculty were collected from the on-line directories of the institution. These 937 e-mail addresses are from the ten colleges and schools of the institution, and owners of these addresses served as the subject population for the study.

Probability sampling was employed for the survey. More specifically, stratified systematic random selection was used to choose potential respondents. That is, a total of 500 e-mail addresses were randomly selected from the total of 937 e-mail addresses. The selection was strat-

---

1. The name of the subject organization is camouflaged in this work to protect the identity of this organization.

ified in terms of the distribution of the e-mail addresses among the ten different colleges and schools of the subject institution. Further description of the survey administration process is offered in later sections of the chapter. Probability sampling was used for two reasons. First, since the study aims to investigate how widespread the phenomenon of public secrets is, it would be desirable for the study results to promise generalizability. In this respect, probability sampling enjoys an apparent advantage over non-probability sampling. Second, probability sampling permits the use of statistical tests to search for group differences, such as those between males and females or those between tenured and non-tenured faculty. Thus, probability sampling facilitates statistical analysis of the survey results, especially results involving participants' demographic information. Non-probability sampling, however, does not allow inferential statistics (Rodeghier, 1996). In addition, this study has an intention to investigate whether differences exist between different groups in terms of their practice of public secrets. Therefore, probability sampling was employed.

The sampling size for this study was determined to be a minimum of 300. Any sampling size that is short of including every member of the subject population represents less complete information of the total population. Of course the larger the sample, the less the sampling error. Yet there is a trade-off in increased cost versus reduction in error. It is up to the researcher to decide where this trade-off should be positioned. According to Rodeghier's (1996, p. 36) formula for calculating the sampling size, the sample equals 1/(acceptable error)^2 *. A sample size of 300 will put the sampling error at 5.8%, a sampling size of 600 will put the sampling error at 4.0%, and a sampling size of 937 would be a complete inclusion of the subject population in the case of this study. Since a difference of 1.8% (5.8%–4.0%) in sampling error does not seem to be significant (Rodeghier, 1996) for this study and a sampling size of 300 is much more economical than one of 600 (especially with consideration of the need of coding open-ended answers), the

---

*　Unusable responses not included.

sampling size for this study is therefore determined at a level of 300, with a sampling rate of 32%.

Regarding the interviews for the study, ten participants were selected. These subjects were people I either personally knew or people who indicated, in their e-mail responses to me, a dislike of the survey method and/or an interest in an interview. For a better representativeness of the subject population, the ten interviewees were selected from the ten different colleges and schools of the subject institution. The interview process and outcomes are explained later on in this chapter.

DESIGN OF THE SURVEY INSTRUMENT AND THE INTERVIEW PROTOCOL

Since I did not find published survey instruments on public secrets or relevant issues, I had to design a survey instrument for this study. The basic underlying framework for designing the survey instrument emanated from the research questions established for the study. Selection of variables and design of measurement scales are based on research literature, results from preliminary interviews and pilot studies.

As established at the beginning of this chapter, there are five research questions for the study. Accordingly, there are five corresponding sections in the survey instrument besides the usual demographics section.

To test and improve the validity and reliability of the survey instrument and the interview protocol, the initial versions were given to ten people for their input about the design and format of the survey instrument and the interview protocol. After incorporation of feedback and suggestions from these people, the survey instrument and interview protocol were submitted to the dissertation committee as an appendix to the dissertation prospectus. After incorporation of modifications and revisions suggested by the committee, I sent the instruments out to 30 professors on the campus of the subject institution as a pilot study. These professors were selected mainly because of their expertise on research methodology. I received feedback from 14 of them about the design and format of the instruments. Although responses from these people turn out to be contradictory sometimes, every effort was made to incorporate their responses into revision of the instrument as I will more specifically explain in this section. In designing the survey instrument, I also made a conscious effort to incorporate ideas from relevant literature, especially those of Ryan and Oestreich (1991), Anthanassiades (1973), Vogel (1967), Gibb (1961), Sefton (1999), and Nonaka and Takeuchi (1995).

As suggested by results from the pilot study, the instructions at the beginning of the survey instrument needed to be clearer through more detailed description of how participants' anonymity and confidentiality are protected. Thus, explanation in this respect was provided in the revised version of the survey instrument. With the help of Web technology, this explanation was also demonstrated with a sample response (reference may be made to http://www.geocities.com/xin-an/ PublicSecretsSurvey.htm). This demonstration through Web technology proved very helpful in offering participants psychological ease and safety. The demonstrable result from this is the comparatively high response rate (64%) for my on-line survey, as can be seen in Chapter Four.

Section one of the survey instrument (please refer to Appendix A) sought to answer research question one: "Does the communication phenomenon of public secrets exist, and, if yes, how widespread is this phenomenon?" More specifically, the first two questions in the survey instrument intended to determine, largely through yes-no responses, whether the phenomenon of public secrets exists. The rest of section one intended to determine how widespread the phenomenon is through responses to 11 items on a six-point scale. Space for comments was provided to solicit further ideas and comments on research question one.

More specifically, question one of the survey instrument was designed in terms of personal and non-personal/formal relationships in the subject's communication, with the former including colleagues, friends, and family; and the latter referring to administrators. This configuration between personal and non-personal relationships or between informal and formal relationships was based on conventional understanding. Question two was designed in terms of the subject's communicational contexts, the private and the public. Question three was designed to help determine the general frequency of the practice of public secrets by contrasting subjects' communication in the informal context and their non-communication in the formal context. The contrast between questions four and five intended to reflect the dichotomy between the public side and the secret side of public secrets, and to determine where subjects' communication is manifested and where it is camouflaged. Selection of the variables of family, friends, colleagues, low level administration, and high level administration were based on a combination of conventional understanding, results from informal, preliminary interviews, and the pilot study.

Regarding section one of the survey instrument, input from the pilot study suggested that the term "organization" was vague and thus was changed into the actual name[2] of the subject institution. The original "genuine opinion" was changed into "frank opinion" because, in the perception of the participants in the pilot study, "genuine" reveals a "viewpoint," implying that selective presentation of views is "not genuine" or "dishonest." "Low administrators" and "high administrators" were vague according to feedback from the pilot study and thus more specification was given to the terms. That is, low level administration was specified as "associate dean and under" and "high level administration" was specified as "dean and higher." Similar changes were made to every section of the survey instrument. The original "other" categories were deleted because participants in the pilot study believed that few respondents would fill out the "other" section. Instead, blank space was provided at the end of each section for respondents' further comments.

---

2. To protect the identity of the subject organization, the actual name of the organization has been camouflaged. Similarly hereafter.

Regarding the measurement scale for this section, terms such as "very often," "often," and "sometimes," in the opinion of five participants in the pilot study, lack inter-subject agreement on what they exactly refer to, thus these terms were changed into more objective and less ambiguous terms such as "more than twice a day" and "more than twice a week." "Always" and "never" were maintained as the anchoring end-points for the scale. Also, as suggested by feedback from the pilot study, the five-point scale was changed to a six-point scale because respondents have a tendency to choose the middle point, especially when it is "sometimes." This was done for another reason. Since input from the pilot study suggested that there was a great difference between "never" and "more than twice a month," "occasionally" was inserted between the two as an intermediate, thus making the scale a six-point one.

Section two of the survey instrument intended to answer research question two: "What factors, in respondents' perception, contribute to the emergence of public secrets?" Seven variables were given to represent factors that may contribute to the emergence of public secrets. A four-point scale was used to determine how important each factor is in contributing to the production of the phenomenon. Space for comments was designed at the end of section two to solicit further ideas on research question two.

According to Ryan and Oestreich (1991), Anthanassiades (1973), and Vogel (1967), fear may cause people to avoid discussing certain topics. In other words, fear may lead to the emergence of "undiscussables" which is a manifestation of public secrets. Fear may be of many kinds. The two major types of fear, as revealed in my informal conversations and interviews with people, are "fear of losing my job" and "fear of penalty from administration," which were selected as the first two variables to represent possible causes of public secrets. Anthanassiades (1973) suggests culture of secrecy as a possible cause of "undiscussables" and thus "culture of secrecy" was also selected as another variable/factor which may lead to the emergence of public secrets. The

rest of the variables in section two of the survey instrument ("suggestions not acknowledged with actions," hierarchy and/or social stratification," "social desirability," and "lack of opportunities to interact,
personally or otherwise, with target audience") were either confirmed
or suggested in the pilot study.

Original instructions for section two were too telegraphic to be easily understandable, as indicated by feedback from the pilot study.
More detailed instructions were plugged into the section. Instructions
were also rephrased in such a way as to avoid a preconceived "viewpoint." Similar changes were made to other sections of the survey
instrument.

Section three of the survey instrument sought answers to research
question three: "What do respondents perceive as the impact of public
secrets on organizational health and organizational members' quality of
work?" Five variables, which represent possible consequences from the
phenomenon of public secrets, were provided to measure subjects' perception. The four-point scale was designed to determine how severe
each possible consequence is. Again, space was provided at the end of
the section to solicit further comments on possible consequences from
an organizational culture that contains a high level of public secrets.

According to Gibb (1961), defensive behavior leads to losses in
communication efficiency, particularly information/communication
distortion, thus defensive behavior leads to a bad communication climate. In practicing public secrets, people apparently attempt to defend
themselves through avoiding certain topics in certain communication
contexts, thus "bad communication climate" was selected as a variable
to represent one possible consequence from public secrets. According
to Sefton's (1999) study, there exists a correlation between dissatisfaction in communication on one hand, and low morale and negative
feelings about the organization on the other. Hence, "low morale" and
"negative feelings about the organization" were selected as two other
variables to represent possible consequences from the phenomenon of
public secrets. "Negative impact on quality of work" and "consider-

ation of relocating a new job" were suggested as other possible consequences through my informal conversations and informal interviews with people.

Section four of the survey instrument sought to answer research question four: "In what areas do public secrets exist?" Six areas or topics were suggested to measure respondents' perception. A seven-point scale was provided to determine how frequently public secrets may occur in each area or topic. Again, space was provided at the end of the section to obtain further comments on areas or topics where public secrets may occur. Original terms not appropriately applicable to a university setting (such as "management," "co-worker") were changed into terms that are more appropriate for a university setting (terms such as "administration" and "colleague"). Vague terms such as "organization" were specified into the actual name of the subject institution.

Besides variables suggested in the pilot study, variables in section four were designed to operate as a tallying reflection of possible causes of public secrets (as in section two of the survey instrument). The rationale was that certain causes of public secrets may lead people to avoid topics that pertain to these causes. More specifically, "administration practices" in section four parallel "fear of penalty from administration" in section two. "Problems at your institution" and "suggestions for improvement of your institution" attempted to parallel "suggestions not acknowledged with actions" since problems are a general motivator of suggestions. "Colleague performance" attempted to tally with "social desirability" in section two since criticism against one's colleagues was not usually considered socially desirable. "Compensation and benefits" is also one of the socially sensitive topics and was thus included as another variable to represent topics avoided in formal discussion. "Well-accepted assumptions that do not work toward the health of your institution" was selected as a variable since well-accepted assumptions are often not included in formal discussion because criticism against well-accepted assumptions does not easily receive ready ears.

Section five of the survey instrument sought to answer research question five: "How effective, in respondents' perception, are the suggested strategies to alleviate the phenomenon of public secrets?" Six strategies were suggested. A four-point scale was designed to determine the effectiveness of each suggested strategy. Space was provided at the end of the section to solicit further comments and more strategies to allay the phenomenon of public secrets.

Selection of variables in this section was based on a combination of research literature, results from the pilot study, and considerations in previous sections of the survey instrument. Nonaka & Takeuchi (1995) suggest a set of strategies to increase knowledge creation within an organization. These strategies include suggestion boxes, free-discussion channels on computer network, and joint meetings involving both organizational members and management. Thus, these strategies were included in section five of the survey instrument to represent possible strategies to increase free expression. Emergence of public secrets obviously has something to do with suppression of criticizing voices. "Reward of criticizing voices" was originally included in the survey instrument. Yet as suggested by results from the pilot study, reward of only criticizing voices may lead to an imbalanced prosperity of complaints and negative opinions with a neglecting of constructive voices. Thus, "reward of criticizing voices" was changed to "reward of active voices." As elaborated previously, public secrets involve taboos and "undiscussables." In this sense, discussion of "undiscussables," especially when the discussion is initiated by administration, may prove an effective strategy to alleviate public secrets. Conventional wisdom has it that organizational members feel nonchalant about offering their suggestions because they believe their suggestions will not be acknowledged with actions. Therefore, "acknowledgement of suggestions with actions as well as with words" was included as another variable or strategy to increase free expression.

The last section of the instrument was the demographics section. Information solicited for this section, more importantly, can be used to determine various correlations and differences between/among groups which may produce food of thought for future research. More specifically, "sex" was included as a demographic variable to help determine whether there exist differences between men and women in their practice of public secrets. "Years of work experience at your institution," "salary range," "tenure," and "academic rank" were included with the hypothesis that these variables may have a correlation with participants' practice of public secrets. "Race/ethnicity" was included as required by general practice, yet there were too few respondents in race categories other than "Caucasian" (as reported in Chapter Four) to enable a valid comparison among different races in terms of their practice of public secrets. "Academic unit" was included to enable a study of possible differences among different colleges and schools of the subject institution.

The demographics section was originally included at the beginning of the survey instrument. Many participants in the pilot study suggested that the demographics section be included at the end instead. Their rationale was that the researcher should not keep respondents guessing his/her hypothesis with regard to the demographic questions as they were filling out the survey. Other changes were also made as a result of the pilot study. For instance, "years of all your work experience" was ambiguous in that it can mean either any work experience or experience only in academia or at the subject institution. Thus, for more clarity and specification, "years of all your work experience" was changed into "total years of your work experience at your institution (including experience as a TA)." Salary ranges were adjusted because the pilot study revealed that few faculty members made under $30,000 a year. The question about salary range was also made optional because some participants in the pilot study perceived it as too intrusive. "Rank" was changed into "academic rank" to avoid confusion with other types of rank such as "administrative rank."

Besides the survey instrument, a protocol (see Appendix D) was developed for the interviews which served as a validation of the survey process and results. The construction of the interview protocol was largely based on the framework of the survey instrument. Yet it was rephrased in such a way as to facilitate solicitation of participants' ideas concerning their practice of public secrets and their perception of others' practice of public secrets. More specifically, questions one, two, and three in the interview protocol paralleled the first section of the survey instrument. Question four paralleled the second section of the survey instrument. Question five paralleled the third section of the survey instrument. Question six paralleled the fourth section of the survey instrument. And question seven reflected the fifth section of the survey instrument. The demographics questions for the interview protocol were the same as those of the survey instrument.

Cronbach alpha coefficients were used to test the reliability of measurement components of the survey instrument. Generally, when only a simple concept such as age or gender is to be measured, only one question needs to be asked. But for more complicated concepts such as "practice of public secrets," a set of several items need to be measured. Cronbach alpha coefficients is the usual method used to measure whether a scale is reliable, or, in other words, whether a multi-item scale is one that produces consistent results when given to the same individual more than once or produces consistent results when given to two or more persons with the same attitude toward the underlying concept (Rodeghier, 1996). As a result of the previously explained efforts in testing and improving the reliability of the survey instrument, the following Cronbach alpha coefficients were obtained for different components in the survey instrument: .80 for the first half of section one (practice of public secrets), .72 for the second half of section one (contrast between informal and formal communications), .82 for section two (causes of public secrets), .85 for section three (consequences from public secrets), .94 for section four (topics in public secrets), and .70 for section five (strategies to alleviate public secrets). These values are satisfactory with the consideration that the general guideline used is to require a Cronbach alpha of 0.70 or above (Rodeghier, 1996).

USE OF WEB TECHNOLOGY

The survey instrument for this study was put on the World Wide Web with an intention to experiment with the Web form as a survey tool. The respondent could directly fill out the survey on the Web by clicking their choices or keying in their comments. After completion, the respondent could send their responses directly into the researcher's e-mail box. Responses appeared in the researcher's e-mail box as coded in numbers. The Web form as a survey tool is relatively new and thus merits more experimentation and investigation. Hypothetically, this survey tool promises unique advantages and yet also contains inherent risks.

First, an on-line survey is more economical because it eliminates postage and duplication costs. It is also more efficient in that electronic mail is much quicker than the traditional postal mail and easier for subjects who are comfortable with electronic mail.

Second, an on-line survey provides complete protection of participants' identification. Responses sent through a Web Form Monitor will completely block the e-mail address and identification of the sender. E-mail addresses sent through the "bcc" function also completely conceal these addresses from the receivers of the message. Consequently, survey participants do not know who among their colleagues are also included in the survey population and are likely to have more psychological safety and ease in responding to the survey. This helps increase the willingness of the participants to respond to the survey.

Third, in terms of data entry, an on-line survey contributes to data accuracy and ease of data analysis. Responses sent to the researcher's e-mail box are electronically stored, can be saved as text format files, and thus are easily transportable into a survey software such as SPSS. This helps decrease data error that may be caused by manual entry.

Fourth, an on-line survey also helps compensate for the inherent deficiency of the impoverished standardization of the survey instrument which can restrain participants' responses. That is, the greater ease to key in words electronically than to write manually may make participants more willing to supply comments if the design of the instrument is confusing or does not suit their individual cases.

Finally, the major risk inherent in an on-line survey is potentially low response rate. In the case of an on-line survey, the researcher is unable to track those who have not responded to the survey. Although sending the survey a second time to all selected subjects could help solve this problem, participants may perceive this practice as "spam" or junk mail. A resulting unpleasant feeling may cause some participants to deliberately refuse to respond to the survey if they have not responded to the survey in the first place. In addition, because the participants' e-mail addresses must generally be acquired from their institution's on-line directories, the sampling can be affected if the directories do not contain current e-mail addresses for employees or continues to list address of people who are no longer working at the institution.

These hypotheses are tested in Chapter Five against the findings of the study.

SURVEY PROCEDURE AND OUTCOMES

The survey for this study was administered electronically except in a few instances when the survey was sent through conventional mail. This was done because a few respondents indicated a preference for conventional mail over electronic mail. As mentioned previously, 937 e-mail addresses were acquired from the subject institution's on-line directory. These e-mail addresses were distributed among ten different colleges and schools of the subject institution. As seen in Appendix B which provides a summary of the survey administration, the survey was completed in three steps. First, 400 e-mail addresses were selected proportionately and randomly from the ten colleges and schools of the subject institution. A cover letter was electronically sent to these 400 people, informing them of the URL link of the on-line survey and instructing them how to complete the survey. The first contact with the selected subjects produced 203 responses in a period of about two weeks.

As the second step, the 400 selected subjects were contacted a second time and a total of 57 additional responses were collected. As the third step, in an effort to reach the planned minimum sample size of 300, another 100 e-mail addresses were selected proportionately and randomly from among the unused e-mail addresses that were distributed in the ten colleges and schools of the subject institution. Contact with these additional 100 subjects produced 62 responses. Among all the 322 responses, 45 responses contained comments of various lengths as answers to the open-ended questions in the survey instrument. So altogether, the survey was sent out to 500 people and 322 responses were obtained with a response rate of 64.4%. Fourteen responses were deleted either because there were many missing values in the responses or because the respondent did not belong to the target population as explained previously in this chapter (Please note that these 14 responses were excluded in Appendix B).

Although responses were sent into my e-mail box and thus were electronically stored, a second independent reader spent hours checking the accuracy of the data, determining missing values in responses, and detecting wrong or unusable answers. This was done to increase validity and reliability of the survey data.

INTERVIEW PROCEDURE AND OUTCOMES

After completion of the survey administration, ten faculty members from the subject institution were selected and interviewed (Appendix D includes the demographic survey form and the guide questions for the interview). They were selected because they indicated, in their e-mail responses to me during the survey administration, a dislike of the survey method and/or an interest in an interview.

These interviews were done in place of the originally planned focus groups. This replacement occurred because of repeated difficulty in scheduling the focus groups, one for tenured and one for untenured faculty. More importantly, subjects were willing to commit to an individual interview, but hesitant to attend a focus group session. Many of them suggested that they might feel uncomfortable talking about "public secrets" in a focus group with people they probably knew which is in itself an interesting finding about people's perception about public secrets.

The interviews served the purpose intended for the focus groups well or even better. Demographically, the interviewees were selected in such a manner so that they could be as close as possible to the original plan for the focus groups. That is, five of the interviewees were tenured faculty and the other five were untenured faculty. They were selected from ten different colleges and schools for optimum representativeness. The purpose of the focus groups was to solicit, from individual respondents, ideas and perceptions not affected by the restraining format of the survey instrument, which could serve as a validation of the survey results. Interviews are in no inferior position or even in a better position to achieve this purpose. As suggested previously, the contacted subjects felt freer to express themselves frankly in an interview than in a focus group. Thus, interviews turned out to be a better method for soliciting subjects' authentic ideas and, therefore, a better validation of the survey process and results. The interviews also promised better to supply richer data for three reasons: (1) The interview is a discovery procedure, but the focus group is not; (2) Participants felt freer in their expressions in individual interviews than in focus group sessions; and (3) The ten interviews were done individually with a greater total amount of time than with the case of two focus groups.

To provide a "safe" environment to the interviewees, all interviews were conducted in the interviewee's office. I first explained the purpose of the study to each interviewee. Then he/she read and signed the informed consent form. After that, I answered any questions each had about the interview. Relevant portions of the interviews were audio-taped and later transcribed. Notes were also taken during the interview. Using a standardized coding scheme, a second person independently coded the transcriptions. Roughly 80% of our coding tallied. Results and discussion of the results from the interviews are respectively presented in Chapters Four and Five.

To sum up, this study utilized Triangulated research methods that involved case illustrations, surveys and interviews. The main rationale behind the adoption of such a methodology is that the three methods complement each other's strengths and compensate for each other's deficiencies as explained in more detail in previous sections of this chapter. To recapitulate the rationale, case illustrations are an effective way to explain a phenomenon that already exists in people's empirical experience since illustrations offer a more concrete and holistic understanding of a phenomenon. Case illustrations were employed to facilitate a better understanding of the phenomenon of public secrets. The survey method was utilized to give scope and breadth to the data for the study. The interviews served as "reconnaissance" and validation for the survey process and results, and they helped to assure better overall validity and reliability for the study by compensating for restrictions of the survey method.

4

RESULTS

PARTICIPANT RESPONSE

A total of 322 faculty members (64.4% of the sampled population of 500) responded to the survey. Among these responses, 308 (61.6% of the sampled population) were usable. The rest were deleted either because the respondents did not answer many questions or because they were not the intended population as explained in Chapter Three.

As the demographics summary shows in Table 4.1, of 308 respondents, 212 were male (68.8%), 95 female (30.8%), and one unclassified (.3%). The mean years of respondents' work experience was 12.4, ranging from 0.5 years to 49 years which were mostly spread out among the numbers between 0.5 and 34, SD=9.09. In terms of race, seven were African-American (2.3%), 19 Asian/Pacific Islander (6.2%), 255 Caucasian (82.8%), six Hispanic (1.9%), and 21 unclassified (6.8%). Regarding salary range, 56 reported a salary under $40,000 (18.2%), 126 reported a salary between $40,000 and $60,000 (40.9%), 119 reported a salary of more than $60,000 (38.6%), and seven did not report their salary (2.3%). In terms of tenure, 180 were tenured (58.4%), 127 untenured (41.2%), and one unclassified (0.3%). Regarding academic rank, 121 were assistant professors (39.3%), 104 associate professors (33.8%), 80 full professors (26.0%), and three unclassified (1.0%). In terms of academic unit, 18 were from the College of Agriculture (5.8%), 25 from the College of Applied Science and Arts (8.1%), 13 from the College of Business and Administration (4.2%), 62 from the College of Education (20.1%), 14 from the College of Engineering (4.5%), 88 from the College of Liberal Arts (28.6%), 12 from the College of Mass Communication and the Media Arts (3.9%), 27 from the College of Science (8.8%), 13 from the School of Law (4.2%), 35 from the School of Medicine (11.4%), and one unclassified (0.3%).

A total of 45 respondents made comments of various lengths as answers to the open-ended questions in the survey (14%). As summarized in Table 4.2, these respondents varied in their demographic backgrounds. Almost every demographic category was represented. Years of respondents' work experience at their institution, the categories of which were too many to be listed in the table, ranged from 1.5 to 31 years, with almost an even distribution among the numbers in between. The mean years of these respondents' work experience was 13.6, SD=8.7.

Ten people were interviewed. Seven interviewees were male (70%). Three were female (30%). Their work experience ranged from 1.5 years to 28 years. In terms of race, eight were Caucasian (80%) and two were Chinese (20%). One reported an annual salary of under $40,000 (10%), four reported a salary of $40,000–$60,000 (40%), and five reported a salary of more than $60,000 (50%). Five interviewees were tenured (50%), and the other five were untenured (50%). Five were assistant professors (50%), two were associate professors (20%), and three were full professors (30%). These interviewees were from ten different colleges and schools of the subject institution (see Table 4.3).

Table 4.1

<u>**Demographics of Survey Respondents**</u>

Demographic categories	Sub-categories	Count	Percent
Sex	male	212	68.8%
	female	95	30.8%
	unclassified	1	0.3%
Race	African-American	7	2.3%
	Asian/Pacific Islander	19	6.2%
	Caucasian	255	82.8%
	Hispanic	6	1.9%
	unclassified	21	6.8%
Salary	under $40,000	56	18.2%
	$40,000–$60,000	126	40.9%
	over $60,000	119	38.6%
	unclassified	7	2.3%
Tenure	tenured	180	58.4%
	untenured	127	41.2%
	unclassified	1	0.3%
Academic rank	assistant professor	121	39.3%
	associate professor	104	33.8%
	full professor	80	26.0%
Academic unit	C. of Agriculture	18	5.8%
	C. of Applied Sciences & Art	25	8.1%
	C. of Business & Administration	13	4.2%
	C. of Education	62	20.1%
	C. of Engineering	14	4.5%
	C. of Liberal Arts	88	28.6%
	C. of Mass Comm. & Media Arts	12	3.9%
	C. of Science	27	8.8%
	School of Law	13	4.2%
	School of Medicine	35	11.4%
	unclassified	1	0.3%

Table 4.2
<u>**Demographics of Respondents Who Answered Open-ended**</u>
<u>**Questions in the Survey**</u>

Demographic categories	Sub-categories	Count	Percent
Sex	male	30	66.7%
	female	15	33.3%
Race	African-American	2	4.4%
	Caucasian	37	82.2%
	Chinese	2	4.4%
	unclassified	4	8.9%
Salary	under $40,000	9	20.0%
	$40,000–$60,000	21	46.7%
	over $60,000	13	28.9%
	unclassified	2	4.4%
Tenure	tenured	28	62.2%
	untenured	17	37.8%
Academic rank	assistant prof.	15	33.3%
	associate prof.	22	48.9%
	full prof.	8	17.8%
Academic unit	C. of Agriculture	6	13.3%
	C. of Applied Sciences & Art	2	4.4%
	C. of Business & Administration	2	4.4%
	C. of Education	7	15.6%
	C. of Engineering	4	8.9%
	C. of Liberal Arts	19	42.2%
	C. of Science	2	4.4%
	School of Law	1	2.2%
	School of Medicine	2	4.4%

Table 4.3
Demographics of the Interviewees

Demographic categories	Sub-categories	Count	Percent
Sex	male	7	70%
	female	3	30%
Race	Caucasian	8	80%
	Chinese	2	20%
Salary	under $40,000	1	10%
	$40,000–$60,000	4	40%
	over $60,000	5	50%
Tenure	tenured	5	50%
	untenured	5	50%
Academic rank	assistant prof.	5	50%
	associate prof.	2	20%
	full prof.	3	30%

RESEARCH QUESTION ONE

RQ1: Does the communication phenomenon of public secrets exist, and, if yes, how widespread is this phenomenon?

The first section of the survey instrument sought to answer research question one. Ten survey items address research question one (see Appendix A for the survey instrument). More specifically, the first two questions were designed to determine whether the phenomenon of public secrets in an organizational setting exists. The third question was to determine the degree of the existence of this phenomenon. Question four was designed to investigate whether there is a difference between faculty's frankness with personal relationships and their frankness with administration. Question five was designed to investigate whether there is a difference between faculty's lack of frankness with personal relationships and their lack of frankness with administration. Results for this section are summarized in Tables 4.4, 4.5, and 4.6.

As indicated in Table 4.4, to the question, "Do you express and exchange frank opinions about your institution with colleagues, friends, and/or family, but not with administrators," 259 responses reported "yes" (84.1%), 47 reported "no"(15.3%), and two reported "do not know"(.6%). This finding demonstrates the existence and a widespread existence of the phenomenon of public secrets in terms of the dichotomy between personal relationships and non-personal relationships (or administration, in the case of this study).

Table 4.4
Existence of "Public Secrets"

	*F-Personal**		*F-Private**	
Responses	frequency	%	frequency	%
Yes	259	84.1	235	76.3
No	47	15.3	65	21.1
Sometimes			8	2.6
Do not know	2	0.6		
Total	308	100%	308	100%

Note.
* Please refer to Appendix C for explanations of the survey codes.

To the question, "Do you express and exchange frank opinions about your institution privately, but not publicly (e.g., at meetings)," 235 responses reported "yes" (76.3%), 65 reported "no" (21.1%), and eight reported "sometimes" (2.6%). This finding reveals the existence of public secrets in terms of the dichotomy between private and public expressions.

As shown in Table 4.5, all respondents believed that they expressed, at least occasionally, frank opinions about their institution informally, but not publicly. Two hundred and ninety respondents reported that they did this more than twice a month (94.2%). This finding confirms the discovery facilitated through previous questions of the survey instrument. That is, the phenomenon of public secrets does exist in this organizational setting, and does so with a compelling severity.

Also as indicated in Table 4.5, 76 respondents (24.7%) reported that they never expressed frank opinions about their institution with low level administrators (associate dean and lower), and 191 respondents (62.0%) reported that they never expressed frank opinions about their institution with high level administrators (dean and higher). In obvious contrast, only nine respondents (2.9%) reported that they never expressed frank opinions about their institution with family; with friends, only 11 reported so (3.6%); and with colleagues, merely one reported so (0.3%). This finding corroborates discoveries through previous questions. More specifically, I found that there is a clear contrast between faculty's frankness with personal relationships (family, friends, and colleagues) and their frankness with administration. That is, faculty are clearly more frank with their personal relationships than with administrators in expressing their opinions about their institution.

Table 4.5

<u>**Communication in "Public Secrets"**</u>

Audience	Always		More than twice a day		More than twice a week		More than twice a month		Occasion- ally		Never	
	ct[†]	%	ct[†]	%	ct[†]	%	ct[†]	%	ct[†]	%	ct[†]	%
F-Frequency*	10	3.2	60	19.5	159	51.6	61	19.8	18	5.8	0	0
F-Family*	7	2.3	37	12.0	123	39.9	79	25.6	52	16.9	9	2.9
F-Friends*	3	1.0	51	16.6	131	39.3	62	20.1	60	19.5	11	3.6
F-Colleague*	18	5.8	67	21.8	132	42.9	63	20.5	27	8.8	1	0.3
F-LoAdm*	0	0	10	3.2	30	9.7	43	14.0	148	48.1	76	24.7
F-HiAdm*	0	0	1	.3	13	4.2	30	9.7	73	23.7	191	62.0

Note.

[†] Count.

* Please refer to Appendix C for explanations of the survey codes.

Table 4.6 presents distribution of different responses to the question, "To whom and how often do you avoid expressing frank opinions about your institution." Two hundred and six respondents reported that they never avoided frank opinions about their institution with family (66.9%); with friends, 201 reported so (65.3%); and with colleagues, 117 reported so (57.5%). On the other hand, only 48 respondents reported that they never avoid expressing, at least occasionally, frank opinions with low level administrators (15.6%). In other words, 260 respondents reported that they did avoid expressing frank opinions about their institution with low level administration, at least occasionally (84.4%). With high level administrators, only 43 respondents reported that they never avoid frank expression about their institution (14%). That is, 265 respondents reported that they did avoid frank expressions about their institution with high level administrators, at least occasionally (86%). More conspicuously, 103 respondents reported that they "always" avoided frank expressions about their institution with high level administrators (33.4%). Thus, as in conformity with discoveries offered by previous questions, a great discrepancy is discernible between faculty's lack of frankness with personal relationships (family, friends, and colleagues) and their lack of frankness with administrators regarding their expressions about their institution.

Table 4.6
Avoidance in "Public Secrets"

Audience	Always		More than twice a day		More than twice a week		More than twice a month		Occasion-ally		Never	
	ct†	%	ct†	%	ct†	%	ct†	%	ct†	%	ct†	%
A-Family*	0	0	3	1.0	6	1.9	48	15.6	45	14.6	206	66.9
A-Friends*	0	0	5	1.6	11	3.6	45	14.6	46	14.9	201	65.3
A-Colleague*	1	0.3	1	0.3	19	6.2	39	12.7	71	23.1	177	57.5
A-LoAdm*	57	18.5	18	5.8	84	27.3	62	20.1	39	12.7	48	15.6
A-HiAdm*	103	33.4	12	3.9	55	17.9	63	20.5	32	10.4	43	14.0

Note.
† Count.
* Please refer to Appendix C for explanations of the survey codes.

To check the validity of the survey process and results, ten interviews were conducted. Results from these interviews largely validated results from the survey, in terms of research question one. Nine interviewees reported that either they themselves practice public secrets or, in their belief, their colleagues do so (90%). Only one interviewee differed (10%) on this point. To the question, "how often do you think you and your colleagues practice public secrets," one responded with "never" (10%), one responded with "sometimes" (10%), four responded with "often" (40%), one responded with "always" (10%), and three responded with "difficult to measure the frequency" (30%), although they affirmed that they did practice public secrets.

I'd like to digress a little bit with another finding. About ten comments (3%) in the survey also expressed a concern about the difficulty to measure the behavioral frequency of practicing public secrets. More specifically, these respondents reported that it was difficult for them to figure out how often they "avoid" frank opinions. This difficulty occurred despite my definition of "avoidance" in the survey instrument: "'Avoid' here includes, when an idea comes up in your mind, (a) you intentionally refrain from expressing it; (b) you lack an opportunity to express it to the targeted audience; and (c) you feel too nonchalant to express it because you believe such expression results in nothing."

To return from the digression to research question one and to summarize, interview and survey results corroborate each other, both revealing that the phenomenon of public secrets exists, and does so with a compelling degree of severity. There also exists a discrepancy between faculty's frankness or lack of frankness with their personal relationships (family, friends, and colleagues) and their frankness or lack of frankness with administrators. That is, faculty are generally more frank with their personal relationships than with administrators.

RESEARCH QUESTION TWO

RQ2: What factors do respondents perceive as contributing to the emergence of public secrets?

The second section of the survey instrument sought answers to research question two. Seven possible factors were suggested and a four-point scale was used to determine the importance of each factor as a possible cause of public secrets. Results for this section are summarized in Table 4.7.

As shown in Table 4.7, 136 respondents did not think that "fear of losing job" was an important factor contributing to the emergence of public secrets (44.2%). One hundred and seventy one respondents (56%) reported that, to varying degrees, "fear of losing job" was an important factor. "Fear of penalty from administration" was not considered an important factor by 68 respondents (22.1%). However, the majority (240, 77.9%) reported that, to varying degrees, "fear of penalty from administration" was an important factor that contributes to the emergence of public secrets. "Suggestions not acknowledged with actions" was not perceived an important factor by only 35 respondents (11.4%).

Table 4.7
Possible Causes of Public Secrets

Causes	Not important		Somewhat important		Important		Very important	
	count	%	count	%	count	%	count	%
FearJob*	136	44.2	97	31.5	54	17.5	20	6.5
FearPenalty*	68	22.1	26	8.4	176	57.1	38	12.3
Suggest+*	35	11.4	74	24.0	120	39.0	79	25.6
Secrecy*	92	29.9	101	32.8	82	26.6	33	10.7
Hierarchy*	61	19.8	94	30.5	108	35.1	43	14.0
SocDesire*	47	15.3	126	40.9	110	35.7	25	8.1
NoInteract*	8	2.6	38	12.3	157	51.0	104	33.8

Note.
* Please refer to Appendix C for explanations of the survey codes.

Still, the vast majority (273, 88.6%) reported that, to varying degrees, it was an important factor. "Culture of secrecy" as a possible cause was perceived as not important by 92 respondents (29.9%). Again, the majority (214, 70.1%) reported that "culture of secrecy" was an important cause of public secrets to varying degrees. Sixty-one respondents perceived "hierarchy or social stratification" as not important in causing public secrets (19.8%), still leaving the majority (245, 80.2%) reporting that it was important to varying degrees. Two hundred and sixty-one respondents (84.7%) reported that "social desirability" was, to varying degrees, an important factor, with only 47 respondents (15.3%) not perceiving so. Finally, the most important cause of public secrets, as the finding revealed, was "lack of interaction opportunities with administrators." A total of 299 respondents (97%) reported that this cause was important in contributing to the emergence of public secrets. Only eight respondents did not think so (2.6%).

Thus, in the perception of the respondents, the suggested causes of public secrets all contribute to the emergence of public secrets. These factors seem to be in the following order from the highest degree of importance to the lowest: lack of interaction opportunities with administration, suggestions unacknowledged with actions, social desirability, hierarchy or social stratification, fear of penalty from administration, culture of secrecy, and fear of losing job.

The majority of these factors that contribute to the emergence of public secrets were validated by interview results. Eight interviewees (80%) reported that "lack of interaction opportunities with administrators" was an important cause of public secrets. Nine of them (90%) reported that administration needed to put forth more effort to seek suggestions from faculty—"they did not consult us," as they claimed. Twenty-three comments in the survey (7% of survey respondents) emphasized that it was more because of lack of interaction opportunities with administrators rather than avoiding them that causes public secrets. One interviewee commented, "The Board of Trustees (BOT) shows a 'contempt' to faculty by presenting no genuine listening to faculty input." Another interviewee reported, "In the 13 years that I've been here, the BOT has never once come to my college and asked for our opinions." Three comments in the survey expressed a similar idea.

Seven interviewees (70%) perceived social desirability as an important cause of public secrets. One interviewee commented on the "us-against-them" attitude in causing public secrets. She said, "...certainly people hate to be seen as always complaining, but there is a certain amount of pressure to complain about issues that are affecting the department as a whole—an 'us-against-them' attitude. So you see that sometimes it is socially desirable to complain." An objective result of this attitude is that known opinions within the department may become "classified information" to those people perceived as "them" or outsiders.

Seven interviewees (70%) reported that "fear of penalty from administration" lead to public secrets. One interviewee reported that she lost her merit pay for "having and expressing several opinions with which my department chair could not agree." Two comments in the survey also related "horror stories" about "trouble-makers being dealt with." Four other comments in the survey talked about the "network of administrators." That is, administrators are networked and listen to each other well. Expression against a certain administrator may easily get into the ears of this criticized administrator and result in possible penalty upon the criticizer. Gradually, faculty may become too wary to express frank opinions to any administrators.

Six interviewees (60%) reported that they refrained from public expression about their institution sometimes because they believed that they did not have enough influence, and that their expression would result in little difference. Seven comments in the survey reported a similar perception. One interviewee said, "I'm too low on the totem pole to exert any influence. Weight given [to] one's opinions is directly related to the hierarchical position one has." This seems to confirm hierarchy and social stratification as a significant cause of public secrets.

Other causes of public secrets were either confirmed by or reported in the interviews and comments in the survey. Four interviewees (40%) reported that a culture of secrecy could lead to emergence of public secrets. Six interviewees (60%) reported that "fear of losing job" could contribute to emergence of public secrets. Three comments in the survey reported that sometimes one refrains from frank public expression about the organization because such expression may lead to financial loss to the organization. In other words, whistle-blowing is not desirable because it may involve financial loss. Two comments in the survey also talked about the mentality of administrators as a cause of public secrets. The comment read, "Some administrators do not feel 'inclined' to hear alternative viewpoints that just 'might' cause them to change their own opinions. This mentality can cause people to avoid expressing certain opinions."

In summary, regarding possible causes of public secrets, lack of interaction opportunities with the target audience seems to be the most important factor. Concomitant with this is administrators' leadership style. Do administrators show willingness to consult and listen to faculty? Are they open to dissenting viewpoints? Are they serious about faculty input? Do they signal threat or penalty to active and divergent voices? All these factors combine to have influence on the emergence of public secrets. Besides these, the cultural factor of social desirability and the organizational factor of hierarchy and stratification can also lead people to practice public secrets, in the perception of the participants.

RESEARCH QUESTION THREE

RQ3: What do respondents perceive as the impact of public secrets on organizational health and organizational members' quality of work?

The third section of the survey instrument sought answers to research question three. An organizational culture that contains a high level of public secrets potentially leads to various negative consequences upon the organizational health. Five possible consequences were suggested to test respondents' perception and a four-point scale was provided to help determine the severity of each potential consequence. Results for this section are summarized in Table 4.8.

As shown in Table 4.8, 79 (25.6%) respondents reported that public secrets would not lead to negative feelings about the organization. The majority of the respondents (229, 74.4%), however, did believe, to varying degrees, that public secrets could potentially result in negative feelings about the organization. Fifty-two respondents (16.9%) did not perceive low morale on their part as a severe, potential consequence from public secrets. The majority (255, 83.1%) reported that public secrets could result in low morale of various degrees. One hundred and eleven respondents (36%) did not believe that an organizational culture containing a high level of public secrets would negatively impact their quality of work, still with the majority (197, 64%) believing so. Compared with other potential negative consequences, "quality of work" seems least impacted by an organizational culture of public secrets. "Bad communication climate," the next item on the list, however, seems to be the most negative consequence from an organizational culture of public secrets. Two hundred and eighty-one respondents (91%) reported that public secrets potentially would lead to a bad organizational communication climate. Only 27 respondents (8.8%) reported otherwise. In terms of job change as a potential negative consequence from public secrets, 244 respondents (79.5%) reported that an organizational culture of public secrets could potentially lead to a contemplation of or actual job change. Only 63 respondents (20.5%) reported that a climate of public secrets would not lead to contemplation of job change.

Table 4.8
Possible Consequences from a Culture of Public Secrets

Consequences	Not severe		Somewhat severe		Severe		Very severe	
	count	%	count	%	count	%	count	%
BadFeel*	79	25.6	134	43.5	59	19.2	36	11.7
LoMorale*	52	16.9	120	39.0	99	32.1	36	11.7
-WorkQuality*	111	36.0	140	45.5	45	14.6	12	3.9
BadComm*	27	8.8	98	31.8	126	40.9	57	18.5
JobChange*	63	20.5	154	50.0	75	24.4	15	4.9

Note.
* Please refer to Appendix C for explanations of the survey codes.

Survey results demonstrate that "bad communication climate" and "low morale" are the leading potential negative consequences from public secrets in the perception of the survey respondents. This was confirmed by interview results. Nine interviewees (90%) reported that they perceived "bad communication climate" and "low morale" as severe potential consequences from public secrets. Contemplation of job change may be a direct or indirect result from low morale which in turn may result from a bad communication climate. Three interviewees (30%) reported that some of their colleagues, who "saw no future here," were sending out resumes. Four respondents to the survey reported that they themselves were sending out resumes as a result of the bad communication climate at their institution. Another four respondents to the survey reported that they saw some of their colleagues doing so. Eight interviewees (80%) also reported that a climate of public secrets could negatively impact the quality of the university as a whole. They reported that the existence of public secrets signaled a low level of involvement of faculty in the governance of the University. As a result, the quality of the University may suffer because of lack of faculty input, they added. Four of these interviewees cited examples to illustrate the correlation between university quality on one hand and faculty involvement and free expression on the other hand.

To summarize the results for research question three, the majority of the survey respondents and the interviewees perceived that public secrets potentially lead to various negative consequences, including bad communication climate, low morale, contemplation of job change, negative feelings about the organization, negative impact on quality of work, and quality of the university. Among these, "bad communication climate" and "low morale" are the leading potential consequences from public secrets.

RESEARCH QUESTION FOUR

RQ4: In what areas do public secrets exist?

Section four of the survey instrument sought answers to research question four which explores the topics that organizational members tend to avoid discussing in formal/public settings. Six topics were suggested to facilitate participants' responses, and a six-point scale was provided to help determine how often faculty members tend to avoid a certain topic in formal/public settings. Results for this section are summarized in Table 4.9.

Table 4.9
Topics Avoided in Public/Formal Discussion

Frequency		Adm. Practice*	Problem*	Suggestion*	Colleague performance	Benefits*	Assumptions*
Always	count	45	10	10	10	10	10
	%	14.6	3.2	3.2	3.2	3.2	3.2
More than twice a day	count	20	8	9	14	12	14
	%	6.5	2.6	2.9	4.5	3.9	4.5
More than twice a week	count	79	55	46	89	55	59
	%	25.6	17.9	14.9	28.9	17.9	19.2
More than twice a month	count	70	96	105	101	105	101
	%	22.7	31.2	34.1	32.8	34.1	32.8
Occasionally	count	54	86	80	64	78	82
	%	17.5	27.9	26.0	20.8	25.3	26.6
Never	count	39	51	57	29	47	40
	%	12.7	16.6	18.5	9.4	15.3	13.0

Note.
* Please refer to Appendix C for explanations of the survey codes.

As demonstrated in Table 4.9, the majority of the respondents avoid formal/public discussion of the five suggested topics. More specifically, only 39 respondents (12.7%) reported that they never avoid public/formal discussion of administrative practices. The majority of respondents (268, 86.3%) reported that they would avoid public/formal discussion of this topic to varying degrees of frequency. "Problems at your institution" as a topic is avoided in formal/public discussion by 255 respondents (83.4%). Only 51 respondents (16.6%) reported they would not avoid this topic in public/formal discussion. "Suggestions to improve your institution" as a topic is avoided in public/formal discussion, to varying degrees of frequency, by 250 respondents (81.5%). Only 57 respondents (18.5%) reported they would never avoid formal/public discussion of this topic. Among all the topics, "colleague performance" seems to be the topic that is most frequently avoided in public/formal discussion. Two hundred and seventy-eight respondents (90.6%) reported that they would avoid formal/public discussion of colleague performance. Concerning "compensation and benefits," only 47 respondents (15%) reported that they never avoid formal/public discussion of this topic. The majority of the respondents (260, 85%) reported that they avoid, to varying degrees of frequency, formal/public discussion of this topic. The last suggested topic in this section of the survey was "well-accepted assumptions that do not work toward the health of your institution." Again, the majority of the respondents (266, 87%) reported that they avoid, to varying degrees of frequency, formal/public discussion of the topic, leaving only 40 respondents (13%) reporting otherwise. Thus, the survey results reveal that the majority of the respondents avoid formal/public discussion of the six suggested topics, though to varying degrees of frequency. "Colleague performance" seems to be the leading topic that is avoided.

Among the six topics suggested in the survey instrument, four were brought up in the interviews: colleague performance, administration practice, compensation and benefits, and accepted assumptions. Seven interviewees (70%) reported that they would avoid formal/public discussion of colleague performance. Six interviewees (60%) reported that they would avoid formal/public discussion of administration practices and compensation and benefits. Five interviewees (50%) reported that they would avoid formal/public discussion of well-accepted assumptions that did not work for the health of their institution. Other topics that may be avoided in formal/public discussion, according to the interviewees, includ salary discrepancy between faculty and administration, philosophy of governance, core curricula, funds allotment, working conditions, and faculty frustration. Three interviewees (30%) reported that they themselves and some of their colleagues privately complained about the great discrepancy between the salary of the administration and that of the faculty—the former was paid "market salary" while the latter is among the nation's lowest. Four interviewees (40%) reported that, despite informal complaints, they would avoid formal/public expression of disputes about philosophy of governance. These participants suggested that faculty generally believed in shared governance, while many administrators believed in "monopolized governance." One interviewee (10%) reported that he would avoid public/formal complaints about some of the University core curricula, which, in his opinion, were "puffy."

In summary, survey and interview results confirm each other to a large extent. They combine to reveal that there do exist topics that are avoided in formal/public discussion or expression. The leading ones among these topics include colleague performance, administrative practices, compensation and benefits, and philosophy of governance.

RESEARCH QUESTION FIVE

RQ5: Are the suggested strategies to allay the phenomenon of public secrets effective in respondents' perception?

Section five of the survey instrument sought answers to research question five. Six strategies were suggested to facilitate responses, and a four-point scale was provided to help determine the effectiveness of each suggested strategy in respondents' perception. Results for this section are summarized in Table 4.10.

Table 4.10
Strategies to Alleviate Public Secrets

Suggested strategies	Not effective		Somewhat effective		Effective		Very Effective	
	count	%	count	%	count	%	count	%
SuggestBox*	136	44.2	138	44.8	31	10.1	2	0.6
RewardVoice*	71	23.1	165	53.6	60	19.5	10	3.2
CompChannel*	62	20.1	159	51.6	76	24.7	10	3.2
D-Undiscussable*	32	10.4	108	35.1	144	46.8	23	7.5
JointMeet*	42	13.6	129	41.9	113	36.7	23	7.5
W/Action*	1	0.3	15	4.9	182	59.1	110	35.7

Note.
* Please refer to Appendix C for explanations for survey codes.

As indicated in Table 4.10, the least effective strategy to allay the communication climate of public secrets, in the respondents' perception, is "suggestion box." One hundred and thirty-six respondents reported that they did not think it was an effective strategy (44.2%). "Acknowledging suggestions with actions," as conventional wisdom would expect, turned out to be the most effective strategy. Only one respondent (0.3%) did not perceive it as an effective strategy. That is, 307 respondents out of a total of 308 did believe, to varying degrees, that "acknowledging suggestions with actions" was effective in alleviating public secrets. With regard to other suggested strategies, 71 respondents (23.1%) reported that "reward of active voices" is not an effective strategy. The rest (235, 76.9%) reported that it is an effective strategy. "Free discussion channels through computer network" as a strategy was perceived effective by 245 respondents (79.9%), with 20.1% of them not perceiving so. Two hundred and seventy-five respondents (89.6%) reported that "discussion of 'undiscussables' initiated by administration" is an effective strategy to help decrease a communication climate of public secrets, leaving 32 respondents (10.4%) not perceiving so.

Finally, "joint meeting involving both faculty and administration" was perceived an effective strategy by 265 respondents (86.4%), leaving 42 respondents (13.6%) not believing so. In short, the survey results demonstrate that the suggested strategies to alleviate public secrets are effective to varying degrees in respondents' perception. "Suggestion box" turned out to be the least effective and "acknowledging suggestions with actions" was perceived as the most effective strategy.

These results from the survey were confirmed by responses from the interviewees. All of the interviewees (10, 100%) reported that "acknowledging suggestions with actions" was effective in alleviating public secrets. "Suggestion box" was not even brought up by the interviewees as a strategy. When I checked with them about their perception of the effectiveness of "suggestion box," eight interviewees (80%) were rather pessimistic. They believed that talk and suggestions were "rarely useful if unacknowledged with actions." The interviewees' pessimism was also attributed to their belief that the phenomenon of public secrets was almost inherent in a bureaucratic organization which is characterized by hierarchies and stratified structures. "Joint meeting" as a strategy was perceived effective by seven interviewees (70%). "Discussion of 'undiscussables' initiated by administration" was perceived effective by six interviewees (60%).

Besides strategies suggested in the survey instrument, other strategies were recommended by interviewees and comments in the survey. Eight interviewees (80%) and six comments in the survey recommended visionary leadership as a strategy to alleviate the phenomenon of public secrets. Eight interviewees (80%) and eight comments in the survey reported that "a climate of honesty and trust" needed to be established in order to alleviate public secrets. "Shared governance" as a strategy was recommended by eight interviewees (80%) and 11 survey comments. Finally, four interviewees (40%) and three survey comments recommended "stable administration" as a strategy to alleviate public secrets.

To sum up for research question five, among the suggested strategies in the survey instrument, "acknowledging suggestions with actions" turned out to be the most effective, and "suggestion box" was perceived to be by far the least effective. Other strategies recommended by interviewees and commentators to the survey include visionary leadership, climate of trust and honesty, shared governance, and stable administration.

EXAMINATION OF GROUP DIFFERENCES AND CORRELATIONS

Although the research questions set out for this study did not intend a specific investigation of possible group differences, such investigation, made possible by the available survey results, may facilitate future research on the topic of public secrets. Independent sample t-tests were completed in terms of respondents' sex and tenure (Tables 4.11 through 4.20). One-way ANOVA analysis and Bonferroni post hoc tests were completed by the factor of respondents' salary range (Tables 4.21 through 4.29). Pearson correlation analysis was completed regarding possible correlation between respondents' years of work experience and different indexes of "public secrets" (Table 4.30).

Table 4.11 presents t-test results by the factor of respondents' sex regarding their "practice of 'public secrets.'" No significant difference was found between male and female respondents in their general practice of "public secrets" or in their interaction with family, friends, and colleagues where "public secrets" are involved. However, there was a statistically significant difference between male and female respondents in their interaction with administrators. With Levene's test for equality of variances resulting in equal variances assumed, the t-test results revealed that female respondents, compared with their male counterparts, are less frequently frank in their interaction with low level administrators (t=2.57, $d.f.$=304, p < .05, male F-LoAdm[1] mean value=5.03, and female F-LoAdm mean value=4.71). The t-test results also revealed that, in their frank expressions about their institution, female respondents more frequently avoid low level administrators (t=-2.0, $d.f.$=305, p < .05, male A-LoAdm mean value=3.21, and female A-LoAdm mean value=3.61) and high level administrators (t=-2.6, $d.f.$=305, p < .01, male A-HiAdm mean value=2.72, and female A-HiAdm mean value=3,39) than male respondents do.

Table 4.12 presents t-test results by the factor of respondents' sex regarding their perception of the importance of the "causes of 'public secrets.'" With Levene's test for equality of variances resulting in equal variances assumed, the t-test results demonstrated a statistically significant difference between male and female respondents in their perception of all the suggested causes of "public secrets." That is, female respondents tend to have a more concerned perception of the causes of "public secrets" than their male counterparts do. More specifically, regarding the importance of "fear of losing job": t=-3.85, $d.f.$=304, p < .01, male mean value=1.72, and female mean value=2.16. Regarding the importance of "fear of penalty from administration": t=-3.56, $d.f.$=305, p < .01, male mean value=2.47, and female mean value=2.88. Regarding the importance of "suggestions unacknowledged with actions": t=-3.85, $d.f.$=305, p < .01, male mean value=2.65, and female mean value=3.09. Regarding the importance of "culture of secrecy": t=-4.32, $d.f.$=305, p < .01, male mean value=2.03, and female mean value=2.54. Regarding the importance of "hierarchy and social stratification": t=-4.84, $d.f.$=303, p < .01, male mean value=2.26, and female mean value=2.82. Regarding the importance of "social desirability": t=-2.88, $d.f.$=305, p < .01, male mean value=2.27, and female mean value=2.57. Regarding the importance of "lack of interaction opportunities with administration": t=-3.06, $d.f.$=304, p < .01, male mean value=3.08, and female mean value=3.35.

---

1.   See Appendix C for explanations of survey codes. Similarly hereinafter.

Table 4.11

**Independent Samples *t*-test of Indexes
of "Practice of 'Public Secrets'" by Respondents' Sex**

Independent Samples Test

		Levene's Test for Equality of Variances		t-test for Equality of Means					95% Confidence Interval of the Mean	
		F	Sig.	t	df	Sig. (2-tailed)	Mean Difference	Std. Error Difference	Lower	Upper
F-Frequency	E-A	1.839	.176	-.135	305	.893	1.45E-02	.11	-.20	.23
	E-N			-.130	165.192	.897	1.45E-02	.11	-.21	.24
F-Family	E-A	1.436	.232	-.177	304	.859	2.36E-02	.13	-.24	.29
	E-N			-.169	160.846	.866	2.36E-02	.14	-.25	.30
F-Friends	E-A	.187	.666	-1.6	305	.108	.22	.14	-4.87E-02	.49
	E-N			-1.6	178.063	.111	.22	.14	-5.13E-02	.50
F-Colleague	E-A	5.298	.022	.287	305	.774	-3.59E-02	.13	-.28	.21
	E-N			.271	158.531	.787	-3.59E-02	.13	-.30	.23
F-LoAdm	E-A	9.215	.003	2.57	304	.011	-.32	.12	-.57	-7.51E-02
	E-N			2.74	212.588	.007	-.32	.12	-.55	-9.00E-02
F-HiAdm	E-A	1.338	.248	1.46	305	.144	-.15	.11	-.36	5.33E-02
	E-N			1.51	194.701	.133	-.15	.10	-.36	4.75E-02
A-Family	E-A	.023	.880	.126	305	.899	-1.40E-02	.11	-.23	.20
	E-N			.127	183.484	.899	-1.40E-02	.11	-.23	.20
A-Friends	E-A	1.149	.285	.700	305	.484	8.41E-02	.12	-.16	.33
	E-N			.688	173.240	.493	8.41E-02	.12	-.16	.33
A-Colleague	E-A	.256	.613	-1.7	305	.087	.21	.12	-2.98E-02	.44
	E-N			-1.7	165.727	.100	.21	.12	-3.97E-02	.45
A-LoAdm	E-A	3.113	.079	-2.0	305	.046	.40	.20	7.23E-03	.80
	E-N			-2.1	198.663	.039	.40	.19	2.13E-02	.78
A-HiAdm	E-A	.423	.516	-2.6	305	.009	.58	.22	.15	1.02
	E-N			-2.7	193.925	.007	.58	.21	.16	1.00

Note.

1. Please refer to Appendix C for explanations of survey codes.

2. E-A: Equal variances assumed.

3. E-N: Equal variances not assumed.

Table 4.12
Independent Samples *t*-test of Indexes
of "Causes of 'Public Secrets'" by Respondents' Sex

Independent Samples Test

		Levene's Test for Equality of Variances		t-test for Equality of Means					95% Confidence Interval of the Mean	
		F	Sig.	t	df	Sig. (2-tailed)	Mean Difference	Std. Error Difference	Lower	Upper
FearJob	E-A	6.090	.014	-3.85	304	.000	-.43	.11	-.65	-.21
	E-N			-3.55	150	.001	-.43	.12	-.67	-.19
FearPenalty	E-A	1.690	.195	-3.56	305	.000	-.42	.12	-.65	-.19
	E-N			-3.46	169	.001	-.42	.12	-.66	-.18
Suggest+	E-A	2.824	.094	-3.85	305	.000	-.44	.12	-.67	-.22
	E-N			-3.95	193	.000	-.44	.11	-.67	-.22
Secrecy	E-A	2.639	.105	-4.32	305	.000	-.51	.12	-.74	-.28
	E-N			-4.26	175	.000	-.51	.12	-.74	-.27
Hierarchy	E-A	.797	.373	-4.84	303	.000	-.56	.12	-.79	-.33
	E-N			-4.85	180	.000	-.56	.12	-.79	-.33
SocDesire	E-A	.042	.837	-2.88	305	.004	-.29	.10	-.50	-.09
	E-N			-2.90	183	.004	-.29	.10	-.50	-.09
NoInteract	E-A	.115	.735	-3.06	304	.002	-.28	9.00E-02	-.45	-.10
	E-N			-3.33	219	.001	-.28	8.27E-02	-.44	-.11

Note.
1. Please refer to Appendix C for explanations of survey codes.
2. E-A: Equal variances assumed.
3. E-N: Equal variances not assumed.

Table 4.13 presents *t*-test results by the factor of respondents' sex regarding their perception of "consequences of 'public secrets.'" With Levene's test for equality of variances resulting in equal variances assumed, the *t*-test results revealed no significant difference between male and female respondents in terms of their perception of the consequences of "public secrets."

Table 4.13
Independent Samples *t*-test of Indexes of "Consequences of 'Public Secrets'" by Respondents' Sex

Independent Samples Test

		Levene's Test for Equality of Variances		t-test for Equality of Means						
									95% Confidence Interval of the Mean	
		F	Sig.	t	df	Sig. (2-tailed)	Mean Difference	Std. Error Difference	Lower	Upper
BadFeel	E-A	.325	.569	.625	305	.532	7.29E-02	.12	-.16	.30
	E-N			.625	181.2	.533	7.29E-02	.12	-.16	.30
LoMorale	E-A	.302	.583	-1.757	304	.080	-.20	.11	-.42	2.E-02
	E-N			-1.742	175.0	.083	-.20	.11	-.42	3.E-02
-WorkQuality	E-A	.071	.790	-1.028	305	.305	-.10	9.92E-02	-.30	9.E-02
	E-N			-.997	168.5	.320	-.10	.10	-.30	1.E-01
BadComm	E-A	.828	.364	-1.858	305	.064	-.20	.11	-.41	1.E-02
	E-N			-1.857	180.5	.065	-.20	.11	-.41	1.E-02
JobChange	E-A	.359	.550	-1.711	304	.088	-.17	9.78E-02	-.36	3.E-02
	E-N			-1.788	201.8	.075	-.17	9.36E-02	-.35	2.E-02

Note.

1. Please refer to Appendix C for explanations of survey codes.

2. E-A: Equal variances assumed.

3. E-N: Equal variances not assumed.

Table 4.14 presents *t*-test results by the factor of respondents' sex regarding the frequency of their avoiding certain "topics involved in 'public secrets.'" With Levene's test for equality of variances resulting in equal variances assumed, the *t*-test results revealed significant difference between male and female respondents concerning their avoiding of five topics involved in "public secrets." More specifically, regarding the topic of "administrative practices": t=-2.598, $d.f.$=304, $p < .05$, male mean value=3.26, and female mean value=3.75. Regarding the topic of "well-accepted assumptions": t=-3.507, $d.f.$=303, $p < .01$, male mean value=3.79, and female mean value=4.30. Regarding the topic of "problems at your institution": t=-3.871, $d.f.$=303, $p < .01$, male mean value=3.89, and female mean value=4.46. Regarding the topic of "colleague performance": t=-2.162, $d.f.$=304, p < .05, male mean value=3.71, and female mean value=4.01. Regarding the topic of "suggestions for improvement of your institution": t=-3.919, $d.f.$=304, p < .01, male mean value=3.93, and female mean value=4.50. These t-test results demonstrate that female respondents tend to avoid frank expression in public/formal discussion more frequently than their male counterparts do.

Table 4.14
Independent Samples _t_-test of Indexes
of "Topics Avoided in 'Public Secrets'" by Respondents' Sex

Independent Samples Test

		Levene's Test for Equality of Variances		t-test for Equality of Means						
									95% Confidence Interval of the Mean	
		F	Sig.	t	df	Sig. (2-tailed)	Mean Difference	Std. Error Difference	Lower	Upper
AdmPractice	E-A	.079	.778	-2.598	304	.010	.49	.19	.12	.86
	E-N			-2.641	188.664	.009	.49	.19	.12	.86
Assumptions	E-A	.987	.321	-3.507	303	.001	.51	.15	.22	.80
	E-N			-3.412	170.118	.001	.51	.15	.22	.81
Benefits	E-A	.010	.920	-1.951	304	.052	.29	.15	-2.52E-03	.58
	E-N			-1.852	160.977	.066	.29	.16	-1.91E-02	.60
Problem	E-A	.390	.533	-3.871	303	.000	.57	.15	.28	.85
	E-N			-3.925	184.649	.000	.57	.14	.28	.85
ColegPerform	E-A	.019	.891	-2.162	304	.031	.31	.14	2.77E-02	.59
	E-N			-2.242	198.103	.026	.31	.14	3.72E-02	.58
Suggestion	E-A	3.811	.052	-3.919	304	.000	.57	.15	.28	.86
	E-N			-4.061	197.794	.000	.57	.14	.29	.85

Note.
1. Please refer to Appendix C for explanations of survey codes.
2. E-A: Equal variances assumed.
3. E-N: Equal variances not assumed.

Table 4.15 presents t-test results by the factor of respondents' sex regarding their perception of the effectiveness of "suggested strategies to alleviate 'public secrets.'" With Levene's test for equality of variances resulting in equal variances assumed, the *t*-test results revealed a statistically significant difference between male and female respondents in their perception of the effectiveness of three strategies. More specifically, regarding "reward of active voices": *t*=-1.462, *d.f.*=304, *p* < .05, male mean value=1.97, and female mean value=2.17. Regarding "discussion of undiscussables": *t*=-2.217, *d.f.*=304, *p* < .05, male mean value=2.45, and female mean value=2.66. Regarding "joint meeting involving both faculty and administration": *t*=2.187, *d.f.*=304, *p* < .05, male mean value=2.45, and female mean value=2.23. These *t*-test results revealed that female respondents, compared with their male counterparts, perceive strategies of "reward of active voices" and "discussion of undiscussables" as more effective and the strategy of "joint meeting" as less effective. No significant difference was found between male and female respondents in their perception of the effectiveness of other suggested strategies to alleviate "public secrets."

T-test results by the factor of respondents' tenure are presented in Tables 4.16 through 4.20. Table 4.16 presents *t*-test results concerning respondents' "practice of 'public secrets.'" With Levene's test for equality of variances resulting in equal variances assumed, the *t*-test results revealed no significant difference between tenured and untenured respondents in their general practice of "public secrets." However, in terms of respondents' interaction with administration, a statistically significant difference was found between tenured and untenured respondents. More specifically, regarding "frequency of frank expression with low level administration": *t*=3.006, *d.f.*=304, *p* < .01, tenured mean value=5.02, and untenured mean value=4.66. Regarding "frequency of frank expression with high level administration": *t*=2.091, *d.f.*=305, *p* < .05, tenured mean value=5.55, and untenured mean value=5.34. Regarding "frequency of avoiding frank expression with low level administration": *t*=-4.613, *d.f.*=305, *p* < .01, tenured mean value=2.99, and untenured mean value=3.84. Regarding "frequency of avoiding frank expression with high level administration": *t*=-2.722, *d.f.*=305, *p* < .01, tenured mean value=2.79, and untenured mean value=3.35. Therefore, tenured faculty tend to be more frank with administration than untenured faculty do.

Table 4.15
Independent Samples *t*-test of Indexes
of "Strategies to Alleviate 'Public Secrets'" by Respondents' Sex

Independent Samples Test

		Levene's Test for Equality of Variances		t-test for Equality of Means						
		F	Sig.	t	df	Sig. (2-tailed)	Mean Difference	Std. Error Difference	95% Confidence Interval of the Mean	
									Lower	Upper
SuggestBox	E-A	2.214	.138	-1.462	304	.145	-.12	8.43E-02	-.29	4.26E-02
	E-N			-1.459	177.40	.146	-.12	8.45E-02	-.29	4.35E-02
RewardVoice	E-A	.153	.696	-2.157	303	.032	-.20	9.21E-02	-.38	-1.74E-02
	E-N			-2.231	193.77	.027	-.20	8.90E-02	-.37	-2.30E-02
CompChannel	E-A	.244	.621	.306	304	.760	2.85E-02	9.32E-02	-.15	.21
	E-N			.293	164.19	.770	2.85E-02	9.73E-02	-.16	.22
D-Undiscussable	E-A	4.071	.044	-2.218	304	.027	-.21	9.60E-02	-.40	-2.41E-02
	E-N			-2.304	198.83	.022	-.21	9.24E-02	-.40	-3.07E-02
JointMeet	E-A	.726	.395	2.187	304	.030	.22	1.00E-01	2.19E-02	.42
	E-N			2.213	186.61	.028	.22	9.88E-02	2.38E-02	.41
W/Action	E-A	.272	.802	-.848	305	.397	-5.96E-02	7.03E-02	-.20	7.88E-02
	E-N			-.855	184.81	.393	-5.96E-02	6.97E-02	-.20	7.79E-02

Note.
1. Please refer to Appendix C for explanations of survey codes.
2. E-A: Equal variances assumed.
3. E-N: Equal variances not assumed.

Table 4.16

Independent Samples *t*-test of Indexes
of "Practice of 'Public Secrets'" by Respondents' Tenure

Independent Samples Test

		Levene's Test for Equality of Variances		t-test for Equality of Means						
									95% Confidence Interval of the Mean	
		F	Sig.	t	df	Sig. (2-tailed)	Mean Difference	Std. Error Difference	Lower	Upper
F-Frequency	E-A	.103	.748	.717	305	.474	-7.23E-02	.10	-.27	.13
	E-N			.715	269.116	.475	-7.23E-02	.10	-.27	.13
F-Family	E-A	1.574	.211	.318	304	.751	-3.97E-02	.12	-.29	.21
	E-N			.313	251.567	.755	-3.97E-02	.13	-.29	.21
F-Friends	E-A	1.694	.194	-1.343	305	.180	.17	.13	-8.E-02	.43
	E-N			-1.357	280.619	.176	.17	.13	-8.E-02	.43
F-Colleague	E-A	.731	.393	-.138	305	.891	1.62E-02	.12	-.22	.25
	E-N			-.136	261.350	.892	1.62E-02	.12	-.22	.25
F-LoAdm	E-A	6.063	.014	3.006	304	.003	-.35	.12	-.58	-.12
	E-N			3.061	287.551	.002	-.35	.11	-.58	-.13
F-HiAdm	E-A	8.011	.005	2.091	305	.037	-.21	9.89E-02	-.40	-.01
	E-N			2.185	302.620	.030	-.21	9.46E-02	-.39	-.02
A-Family	E-A	.697	.405	-1.466	305	.144	.15	.10	-5.E-02	.35
	E-N			-1.467	272.751	.144	.15	.10	-5.E-02	.35
A-Friends	E-A	2.025	.156	-.813	305	.417	9.15E-02	.11	-.13	.31
	E-N			-.796	250.270	.427	9.15E-02	.11	-.13	.32
A-Colleague	E-A	.265	.607	-1.925	305	.055	.22	.11	-5.E-03	.44
	E-N			-1.887	250.872	.060	.22	.11	-9.E-03	.44
A-LoAdm	E-A	2.376	.124	-4.613	305	.000	.85	.18	.49	1.21
	E-N			-4.507	247.774	.000	.85	.19	.48	1.22
A-HiAdm	E-A	2.011	.157	-2.722	305	.007	.56	.21	.16	.97
	E-N			-2.692	260.349	.008	.56	.21	.15	.97

Note.

1. Please refer to Appendix C for explanations of survey codes.

2. E-A: Equal variances assumed.

3. E-N: Equal variances not assumed.

Table 4.17 presents *t*-test results by the factor of respondents' tenure regarding their perception of the importance of the "causes of 'public secrets.'" With Levene's test for equality of variances resulting in equal variances assumed, the *t*-test results demonstrated a statistically significant difference between male and female respondents in their perception of five suggested causes of "public secrets." That is, untenured respondents tend to have a more concerned perception of these causes of "public secrets" than tenured respondents do. More specifically, regarding the importance of "fear of losing job": $t=-10.05$, $d.f.=304$, $p < .01$, tenured mean value=1.47, and untenured mean value=2.41. Regarding the importance of "fear of penalty from administration": $t=-5.154$, $d.f.=305$, $p < .01$, tenured mean value=2.37, and untenured mean value=2.92. Regarding the importance of "hierarchy and social stratification": $t=-3.114$, $d.f.=303$, $p < .01$, tenured mean value=2.29, and untenured mean value=2.63. Regarding the importance of "social desirability": $t=-2.604$, $d.f.=305$, $p < .05$, tenured mean value=2.26, and untenured mean value=2.51. Regarding the importance of "no interaction opportunities with administration": $t=-2.401$, $d.f.=304$, $p < .05$, tenured mean value=3.07, and untenured mean value=3.28. No statistically significant difference was found between tenured and untenured faculty concerning their perception of "suggestions unacknowledged with actions" and "culture of secrecy" as causes of "public secrets."

Table 4.17

**Independent Samples *t*-test of Indexes
of "Causes of 'Public Secrets'" by Respondents' Tenure**

Independent Samples Test

		Levene's Test for Equality of Variances		t-test for Equality of Means						
									95% Confidence Interval of the Mean	
		F	Sig.	t	df	Sig. (2-tailed)	Mean Difference	Std. Error Difference	Lower	Upper
FearJob	E-A	6.137	.014	-10.05	304	.000	-.94	9.36E-02	-1.12	-.76
	E-N			-9.739	237.740	.000	-.94	9.66E-02	-1.13	-.75
FearPenalty	E-A	45.244	.000	-5.154	305	.000	-.55	.11	-.77	-.34
	E-N			-5.341	299.084	.000	-.55	.10	-.76	-.35
Suggest+	E-A	.567	.452	-1.567	305	.118	-.17	.11	-.39	4.E-02
	E-N			-1.544	256.042	.124	-.17	.11	-.39	5.E-02
Secrecy	E-A	.169	.681	-.522	305	.602	-5.94E-02	.11	-.28	.16
	E-N			-.528	282.355	.598	-5.94E-02	.11	-.28	.16
Hierarchy	E-A	2.505	.115	-3.114	303	.002	-.34	.11	-.56	-.13
	E-N			-3.164	283.355	.002	-.34	.11	-.56	-.13
SocDesire	E-A	4.218	.041	-2.604	305	.010	-.25	9.63E-02	-.44	-6.E-02
	E-N			-2.558	253.215	.011	-.25	9.80E-02	-.44	-6.E-02
NoInteract	E-A	.271	.603	-2.491	304	.013	-.21	8.47E-02	-.38	-4.E-02
	E-N			-2.566	295.543	.011	-.21	8.22E-02	-.37	-5.E-02

Note.

1. Please refer to Appendix C for explanations of survey codes.

2. E-A: Equal variances assumed.

3. E-N: Equal variances not assumed.

Table 4.18 presents *t*-test results by the factor of respondents' tenure regarding their perception of the severity of the "consequences of 'public secrets.'" With Levene's test for equality of variances resulting in equal variances assumed, the *t*-test results revealed statistically significant difference between tenured and untenured respondents in terms of their perception of only two consequences of "public secrets." That is, regarding "negative impact on work quality": $t=-2.764$, $d.f.=305$, $p <$ .01, tenured mean value=1.76, and untenured mean value=2.02. Regarding "consideration of job change": $t=-4.480$, $d.f.=304$, $p < .01$, tenured mean value=1.97, and untenured mean value=2.37. No significant difference was found between tenured and untenured faculty in terms of their perception of the rest of the consequences of "public secrets."

Table 4.18
Independent Samples t-test of Indexes of
"Consequences of 'Public Secrets'" by Respondents' Tenure

Independent Samples Test

		Levene's Test for Equality of Variances		t-test for Equality of Means					95% Confidence Interval of the Mean	
		F	Sig.	t	df	Sig. (2-tailed)	Mean Difference	Std. Error Difference	Lower	Upper
BadFeel	E-A	4.71	.031	1.365	305	.173	.15	.11	-6.6E-02	.36
	E-N			1.384	284.38	.167	.15	.11	-6.3E-02	.36
LoMorale	E-A	.334	.564	-1.732	304	.084	-.18	.10	-.39	2.E-02
	E-N			-1.731	268.71	.085	-.18	.10	-.39	2.E-02
-WorkQuality	E-A	3.30	.070	-2.764	305	.006	-.25	9.21E-02	-.44	-7.E-02
	E-N			-2.752	267.14	.006	-.25	9.25E-02	-.44	-7.E-02
BadComm	E-A	2.31	.130	.148	305	.883	1.50E-02	.10	-.18	.21
	E-N			.149	278.56	.882	1.50E-02	.10	-.18	.21
JobChange	E-A	5.16	.024	-4.480	304	.000	-.40	8.95E-02	-.58	-.22
	E-N			-4.468	266.59	.000	-.40	8.97E-02	-.58	-.22

Note.
1. Please refer to Appendix C for explanations of survey codes.
2. E-A: Equal variances assumed.
3. E-N: Equal variances not assumed.

Table 4.19 presents *t*-test results by the factor of respondents' tenure regarding the frequency of their avoiding certain topics involved in "public secrets." With Levene's test for equality of variances resulting in equal variances assumed, the *t*-test results revealed statistically significant difference between tenured and untenured respondents in terms of their avoiding three topics involved in "public secrets." More specifically, regarding "administrative practices": $t=-3.272$, $d.f.=304$, $p < .01$, tenured mean value=3.26, and untenured mean value=3.74. Regarding "problems at your institution": t=-2.822, $d.f.$=303, $p < .01$, tenured mean value=4.06, and untenured mean value=4.45. Regarding "suggestions for improvement of your institution": t=-2.262, $d.f.$=304, $p < .05$, tenured mean value=4.13, and untenured mean value=4.45. These t-test results revealed that tenured faculty less frequently avoid the three topics in public/formal discussion than untenured faculty do. No significant difference was found between tenured and untenured faculty in terms of their avoiding the rest of the topics in "public secrets."

Table 4.19
Independent Samples _t_-test of Indexes
of "Topics Avoided in 'Public Secrets'" by Respondents' Tenure

Independent Samples Test

| | | Levene's Test for Equality of Variances | | t-test for Equality of Means | | | | | | |
| | | F | Sig. | t | df | Sig. (2-tailed) | Mean Difference | Std. Error Difference | 95% Confidence Interval of the Mean | |
									Lower	Upper
AdmPractice	E-A	5.457	.020	-3.272	304	.001	.58	.18	.23	.92
	E-N			-3.183	241.485	.002	.58	.18	.22	.93
Assumptions	E-A	7.903	.005	-1.729	303	.085	.24	.14	-3.3E-02	.51
	E-N			-1.657	225.760	.099	.24	.15	-4.6E-02	.53
Benefits	E-A	1.949	.164	-1.655	304	.099	.23	.14	-4.4E-02	.51
	E-N			-1.591	229.490	.113	.23	.15	-5.5E-02	.52
Problem	E-A	7.864	.005	-2.822	303	.006	.39	.14	.12	.66
	E-N			-2.701	224.524	.007	.39	.14	.11	.68
ColegPerform	E-A	15.922	.000	-1.673	304	.095	.23	.13	-4.0E-02	.49
	E-N			-1.599	223.486	.111	.23	.14	-5.2E-02	.50
Suggestion	E-A	4.121	.043	-2.262	304	.024	.32	.14	4.10E-02	.59
	E-N			-2.171	227.874	.031	.32	.15	2.91E-02	.60

Note.
1. Please refer to Appendix C for explanations of survey codes.
2. E-A: Equal variances assumed.
3. E-N: Equal variances not assumed.

Table 4.20 presents *t*-test results by the factor of respondents' tenure regarding their perception of the effectiveness of the suggested "strategies to alleviate 'public secrets.'" With Levene's test for equality of variances resulting in equal variances assumed, the *t*-test results revealed no statistically significant difference between tenured and untenured respondents in terms of their perception of the strategies.

Table 4.20
Independent Samples *t*-test of Indexes
of "Strategies to Alleviate 'Public Secrets'" by Respondents' Tenure

Independent Samples Test

		Levene's Test for Equality of Variances		t-test for Equality of Means						
						Sig.	Mean	Std. Error	95% Confidence Interval of the Mean	
		F	Sig.	t	df	(2-tailed)	Difference	Difference	Lower	Upper
SuggestBox	E-A	.122	.727	-1.123	304	.262	-8.89E-02	7.91E-02	-.24	6.68E-02
	E-N			-1.114	260.954	.266	-8.89E-02	7.98E-02	-.25	6.82E-02
RewardVoice	E-A	1.213	.272	-1.697	303	.091	-.15	8.66E-02	-.32	2.35E-02
	E-N			-1.720	281.246	.087	-.15	8.55E-02	-.32	2.13E-02
CompChannel	E-A	.508	.477	-.091	304	.928	-7.94E-03	8.76E-02	-.18	.16
	E-N			-.091	276.873	.927	-7.94E-03	8.69E-02	-.18	.16
D-Undiscussable	E-A	8.059	.005	-.508	304	.612	-4.61E-02	9.08E-02	-.22	.13
	E-N			-.525	298.201	.600	-4.61E-02	8.77E-02	-.22	.13
JointMeet	E-A	.320	.572	.506	304	.613	4.79E-02	9.46E-02	-.14	.23
	E-N			.504	265.854	.615	4.79E-02	9.51E-02	-.14	.24
W/Action	E-A	.283	.595	-.226	305	.821	-1.50E-02	6.61E-02	-.15	.12
	E-N			-.226	269.949	.821	-1.50E-02	6.62E-02	-.15	.12

Note.
1. Please refer to Appendix C for explanations of survey codes.
2. E-A: Equal variances assumed.
3. E-N: Equal variances not assumed.

Tables 4.21, 4.23, 4.25, 4.27, and 4.29 present one-way ANOVA results by respondents' salary ranges (under $40,000, $40,000–60,000, and over $60,000). Tables 4.22, 4.24, 4.26, and 4.28 present Bonferroni post hoc test results showing significant mean group differences by the factor of salary range.

Table 4.21

One-Way ANOVA of Indexes of Practice of "Public Secrets" by Salary Range

Indexes of Practice of "Public Secrets"		Sum of Squares	df	Mean Square	F	Sig.
F-Frequency[†]	Between groups	10.259	2	5.129	7.131	.001
	Within groups	214.339	298	.719		
	Total	224.598	300			
F-Family[†]	Between groups	.977	2	.488	.715	.490
	Within groups	203.475	298	.683		
	Total	204.452	300			
F-Friends[†]	Between groups	12.350	2	6.175	1.920	.148
	Within groups	958.574	298	3.217		
	Total	970.924	300			
F-Colleague[†]	Between groups	12.072	2	6.036	6.051	.003
	Within groups	297.277	298	.998		
	Total	309.349	300			
F-LoAdm[†]	Between groups	10.568	2	5.284	5.270	.006
	Within groups	297.762	297	1.003		
	Total	308.330	299			
F-HiAdm[†]	Between groups	20.855	2	10.427	9.615	.000
	Within groups	322.092	297	1.084		
	Total	342.947	299			
A-Family[†]	Between groups	1.672	2	.836	1.060	.348
	Within groups	235.059	298	.789		
	Total	236.731	300			
A-Friends[†]	Between groups	3.875	2	1.937	2.152	.118
	Within groups	268.285	298	.900		
	Total	272.159	300			
A-Colleague[†]	Between groups	3.845	2	1.922	2.079	.127
	Within groups	275.537	298	.925		
	Total	279.382	300			
A-LoAdm[†]	Between groups	30.931	2	15.466	5.908	.003
	Within groups	780.079	298	2.618		
	Total	811.010	300			
A-HiAdm[†]	Between groups	8.636	2	4.318	3.510	.031
	Within groups	366.607	298	1.230		
	Total	375.243	300			

[†] Please refer to Appendix C for explanations of survey codes.

To be more specific, Table 4.21 presents results concerning respondents' practice of "public secrets." No significant difference was found regarding respondents' interaction with family and friends. However, regarding other indexes of "practice of 'public secrets,'" statistically significant difference was found. That is, in terms of respondents' "frequency of frank expression informally but not formally": $F=7.131$, $d.f.=2$, $p < .01$. In terms of respondents' "frequency of frank expression with colleagues": $F=6.051$, $d.f.=2$, $p < .01$. In terms of respondents' "frequency of frank expression with low level administration": $F=5.270$, $d.f.=2$, $p < .01$. In terms of respondents' "frequency of frank expression with high level administration": $F=9.615$, $d.f.=2$, $p < .01$. In terms of respondents' "frequency of avoiding frank expression with low level administration": $F=5.908$, $d.f.=2$, $p < .01$. In terms of respondents' "frequency of avoiding frank expression with high level administration": $F=5.908$, $d.f.=2$, $p < .05$. Significant group mean differences concerning respondents' practice of "public secrets" as shown by Bonferroni post hoc test results are presented in Table 4.22. These results revealed that respondents with higher salary ranges tend to be more frank with administration.

Table 4.22
Bonferroni Post Hoc Test Results Showing Significant Mean Differences by the Factor of Salary Range Regarding "Practice of 'Public Secrets"

Indexes	Group Comparison	Significant Mean Difference (p < .05)
F-Frequency[†]	Under $40,000 vs. $40,000–$60,000	-.36
	Under $40,000 vs. over $60,000	
	$40,000–$60,000 vs. over $60,000	-.38
F-Colleague[†]	Under $40,000 vs. $40,000–$60,000	-.47
	Under $40,000 vs. over $60,000	
	$40,000–$60,000 vs. over $60,000	-.36
F-LoAdm[†]	Under $40,000 vs. $40,000–$60,000	
	Under $40,000 vs. over $60,000	
	$40,000–$60,000 vs. over $60,000	-.41
F-LoAdm[†]	Under $40,000 vs. $40,000–$60,000	
	Under $40,000 vs. over $60,000	.72
	$40,000–$60,000 vs. over $60,000	.62

[†] Please refer to Appendix C for explanations of survey codes.

Table 4.23 presents one-way ANOVA results by salary range regarding respondents' perception of the importance of "causes of 'public secrets.'" Statistically significant difference was found only in two causes of "public secrets": fear of losing job and fear of administrative penalty. More specifically, in terms of respondents' perception of the severity of "fear of losing job" as a cause of "public secrets": $F=27.426$, $d.f.=2$, $p < .01$. In terms of respondents' perception of the severity of "fear of administrative penalty" as a cause of "public secrets": $F=5.121$, $d.f.=2$, $p < .01$. One-way ANOVA results revealed no significant difference between the three salary range groups in their perception of other causes of "public secrets." Significant group mean differences concerning respondents' perception of causes of "public secrets" as shown by Bonferroni post hoc test results are presented in Table 4.24. These results revealed that respondents with higher salary ranges tend to have a less concerned perception of the presented causes of "public secrets."

Table 4.23
One-Way ANOVA of Indexes of Causes of "Public Secrets" by Salary Range

Indexes of Causes of "Public Secrets"		Sum of Squares	df	Mean Squaure	F	Sig.
FearJob[†]	Between groups	40.439	2	20.219	27.426	.000
	Within groups	218.958	297	.737		
	Total	259.397	299			
FearPenalty[†]	Between groups	9.250	2	4.625	5.121	.007
	Within groups	269.109	298	.903		
	Total	278.359	300			
Suggest+[†]	Between groups	.448	2	.224	.244	.784
	Within groups	273.592	298	.918		
	Total	274.040	300			
Secrecy[†]	Between groups	1.112	2	.556	.583	.559
	Within groups	284.323	298	.954		
	Total	285.435	300			
Hierarchy[†]	Between groups	.977	2	.488	.715	.490
	Within groups	203.475	298	.683		
	Total	204.452	300			
SocDesire[†]	Between groups	3.157	2	1.578	2.265	.106
	Within groups	207.667	298	.697		
	Total	210.824	300			
NoInteract[†]	Between groups	2.366	2	1.183	2.312	.101
	Within groups	151.964	297	.512		
	Total	154.330	299			

[†] Please refer to Appendix C for explanations of survey codes.

Table 4.24
Bonferroni Post Hoc Test Results Showing Significant Mean Differences by the Factor of Salary Range Regarding "Perception of Causes of 'Public Secrets"

Indexes	Group Comparison	Significant Mean Difference (p < .05)
FearJob[†]	Under $40,000 vs. $40,000–$60,000	.56
	Under $40,000 vs. over $60,000	1.02
	$40,000–60,000 vs. over $60,000	.45
FearPenalty[†]	Under $40,000 vs. $40,000–60,000	
	Under $40,000 vs. over $60,000	.48
	$40,000–60,000 vs. over $60,000	

[†] Please refer to Appendix C for explanations of survey codes.

Table 4.25 presents one-way ANOVA results by salary range regarding respondents' perception of the severity of "consequences of 'public secrets.'" Statistically significant difference was found among the three salary range groups in their perception of all the suggested consequences of "public secrets." More specifically, in terms of "negative feeling about the institution": $F=4.613$, $d.f.=2$, $p < .05$. In terms of "low morale": $F=5.121$, $d.f.=2$, $p < .01$. In terms of "negative impact on work quality": $F=4.860$, $d.f.=2$, $p < .01$. In terms of "bad communication climate": $F=5.222$, $d.f.=2$, $p < .01$. In terms of "consideration of job change": $F=14.988$, $d.f.=2$, $p < .01$. Table 4.26 presents significant group mean differences concerning the three salary range groups' perception of the consequences of "public secrets" as shown by Bonferroni post hoc test results. These results represent mixed findings. Roughly speaking, respondents with higher salary range tend to be less impacted by the phenomenon of "public secrets." However, in terms of "negative feelings about the institution," the "$40,000–$60,000" salary group seems to be more impacted than the "under $40,000" salary group.

Table 4.25
One-Way ANOVA of Indexes of Consequences of "Public Secrets" by Salary Range

Indexes of Causes of "Public Secrets"		Sum of Squares	df	Mean Squaure	F	Sig.
BadFeel[†]	Between groups	7.954	2	3.977	4.612	.011
	Within groups	256.996	298	.862		
	Total	264.950	300			
LoMorale[†]	Between groups	9.250	2	4.625	5.121	.007
	Within groups	269.109	298	.903		
	Total	278.359	300			
-WorkQuality[†]	Between groups	6.102	2	3.051	4.860	.008
	Within groups	187.100	298	.628		
	Total	193.203	300			
BadComm[†]	Between groups	7.565	2	3.783	5.222	.006
	Within groups	215.864	298	.724		
	Total	223.429	300			
JobChange[†]	Between groups	17.075	2	8.537	14.988	.000
	Within groups	169.175	297	.570		
	Total	186.250	299			

[†] Please refer to Appendix C for explanations of survey codes.

Table 4.26
Bonferroni Post Hoc Test Results Showing Significant Mean
Differences by the Factor of Salary Range Regarding
"Consequences of 'Public Secrets"

Indexes	Group Comparison	Significant Mean Difference (p < .05)
BadComm[†]	Under $40,000 vs. $40,000–$60,000	
	Under $40,000 vs. over $60,000	
	$40,000–$60,000 vs. over $60,000	.35
BadFeel[†]	Under $40,000 vs. $40,000–$60,000	-.43
	Under $40,000 vs. over $60,000	
	$40,000–$60,000 vs. over $60,000	
-WorkQuality[†]	Under $40,000 vs. $40,000–$60,000	.31
	Under $40,000 vs. over $60,000	.40
	$40,000–$60,000 vs. over $60,000	
JobChange[†]	Under $40,000 vs. $40,000–$60,000	
	Under $40,000 vs. over $60,000	.35
	$40,000–$60,000 vs. over $60,000	.52

[†] Please refer to Appendix C for explanations of survey codes.

Table 4.27 presents one-way ANOVA results by salary range regarding respondents' frequency of avoiding certain topics in "public secrets." Statistically significant difference was found among the three salary range groups in their avoiding of five topics in "public secrets." More specifically, in terms of "administrative practices": $F=3.285$, $d.f.=2$, $p < .05$. In terms of "problems of the institution": $F=10.550$, $d.f.=2$, $p < .01$. In terms of "suggestions for improvement of the institution": $F=9.155$, $d.f.=2$, $p < .01$. In terms of "bad communication climate": $F=5.222$, $d.f.=2$, $p < .01$. In terms of "benefits and compensation": $F=5.811$, $d.f.=2$, $p < .01$. In terms of "bad communication climate": $F=5.222$, $d.f.=2$, $p < .01$. In terms of "well-accepted assumptions": $F=6.453$, $d.f.=2$, $p < .01$. Table 4.28 presents significant group mean differences concerning certain topics avoided in "public secrets" as shown by Bonferroni post hoc test results. These results revealed that, generally speaking, higher salary range groups tend to be more frequent in avoiding the presented topics than lower salary range groups. However, no significant difference was found between the "under $40,000" salary range group and the "$40,000–$60,000" salary range group.

Table 4.27
One-Way ANOVA of Indexes of Topics in "Public Secrets" by Salary Range

Indexes of Causes of "Public Secrets"		Sum of Squares	df	Mean Squaure	F	Sig.
AdmPractice[†]	Between groups	15.426	2	7.713	3.285	.039
	Within groups	697.320	297	2.348		
	Total	712.747	299			
Problem[†]	Between groups	28.430	2	14.215	10.550	.000
	Within groups	398.834	296	1.347		
	Total	427.264	298			
Suggestion[†]	Between groups	24.674	2	12.337	9.155	.000
	Within groups	400.243	297	1.348		
	Total	424.917	299			
ColegPerform[†]	Between groups	3.831	2	1.915	1.420	.243
	Within groups	400.556	297	1.349		
	Total	404.387	299			
Benefits[†]	Between groups	16.124	2	8.062	5.811	.003
	Within groups	412.046	297	1.387		
	Total	428.170	299			
Assumptions[†]	Between groups	18.000	2	9.000	6.453	.002
	Within groups	412.816	296	1.395		
	Total	430.816	298			

[†] Please refer to Appendix C for explanations of survey codes.

Table 4.28
Bonferroni Post Hoc Test Results Showing Significant Mean Differences by the Factor of Salary Range Regarding "Topics Avoided in 'Public Secrets"

Indexes	Group Comparison	Significant Mean Difference (p < .05)
AdmPractice[†]	Under $40,000 vs. $40,000–$60,000	
	Under $40,000 vs. over $60,000	
	$40,000–$60,000 vs. over $60,000	.48
Problems[†]	Under $40,000 vs. $40,000–$60,000	
	Under $40,000 vs. over $60,000	.70
	$40,000–$60,000 vs. over $60,000	.59
Suggestion[†]	Under $40,000 vs. $40,000–$60,000	
	Under $40,000 vs. over $60,000	.68
	$40,000–$60,000 vs. over $60,000	.53
Benefits[†]	Under $40,000 vs. $40,000–$60,000	
	Under $40,000 vs. over $60,000	.64
	$40,000–$60,000 vs. over $60,000	
Assumptions[†]	Under $40,000 vs. $40,000–$60,000	
	Under $40,000 vs. over $60,000	.52
	$40,000–$60,000 vs. over $60,000	.49

[†] Please refer to Appendix C for explanations of survey codes.

Table 4.29 presents one-way ANOVA results by salary range regarding respondents' perception of the effectiveness of the suggested "strategies to alleviate 'public secrets.'" Statistically significant difference was found among the three salary range groups in their perception of only one strategy: "joint meeting involving both faculty and administration," $F=3.109$, $d.f.=2$, $p < .05$. Regarding this strategy, the mean difference between the "under $40,000" group and the "$40,000–$60,000" group and that between the "under $40,000" group and the "over 60,000" group are both .40, $p < .05$.

Table 4.29
One-Way ANOVA of Indexes of Strategies
to Alleviate "Public Secrets" by Salary Range

Indexes of Causes of "Public Secrets"		Sum of Squares	df	Mean Squaure	F	Sig.
SuggestBox[†]	Between groups	.683	2	.341	1.042	.354
	Within groups	97.583	298	.327		
	Total	98.266	300			
RewardVoice[†]	Between groups	.678	2	.339	.601	.549
	Within groups	166.988	296	.564		
	Total	167.666	298			
CompChannel[†]	Between groups	2.582	2	1.291	2.288	.103
	Within groups	167.565	297	.564		
	Total	170.147	299			
D-Undiscussable[†]	Between groups	1.436	2	.718	1.176	.310
	Within groups	181.350	297	.611		
	Total	182.787	299			
JointMeet[†]	Between groups	4.120	2	2.060	3.109	.046
	Within groups	196.797	297	.663		
	Total	200.917	299			
W/Action[†]	Between groups	.683	2	.341	1.042	.354
	Within groups	97.583	298	.327		
	Total	98.266	300			

[†] Please refer to Appendix C for explanations of survey codes.

Pearson r values were used to test for correlation between respondents' years of work experience and different indexes of "public secrets." The results are presented in Table 4.30. A very slight correlation is discernible between respondents' years of work experience and their practice of public secrets (F-Personal, F-Private). Respondents with more years of work experience tend (a slight tendency though) to be freer in public or formal discussion, which may be explained by their more familiarity with their workplace and possibly also by their tenure as a result of their more years of work at their institution. Respondents with more years of work experience tend to be more frank and thus avoid less low and high level administration [$r(307)$=.242, $p <$ .01; $r(307)$=.255, $p <$ .01]. Also as shown in Table 4.30, respondents with more years of work experience tend to have a less concerned perception of the causes of public secrets. In terms of the perception of possible consequences from public secrets, respondents with more years of work experience are less inclined for a job change. In terms of topics that may be avoided in public/formal discussion, respondents with more years of work experience are slightly more frank in discussing the topics, especially in the case of "administration practices" and "colleague performance." There is no statistically significant correlation between respondents' years of work experience and their perception of the effectiveness of the suggested strategies to alleviate "public secrets."

To sum up, respondents with more years of work experience practice public secrets slightly less, are slightly more frank with administrators, have a slightly lesser perceptionof causes of public secrets, and are slightly more frank with certain topics in public/formal discussion.

Finally, as presented in Table 4.31, no significant differences were found between the ten colleges and schools of the subject institution in their practice of different aspects of "public secrets."

Table 4.30
Pearson *r* Values Representing Correlations and Non-Correlations
Between Respondents' Years of Work Experience and Different
Indexes of "Public Secrets"

	Years of work	
	Pearson correlation coefficients	Significance level
F-Personal[†]	.131[*]	.021
F-Private[†]	.195[**]	.001
F-Frequency[†]	-.012[*]	.038
F-Family[†]	.069	.226
F-Friends[†]	-.044	.442
F-Colleague[†]	-.070	.223
F-LoAdm[†]	.242[**]	.000
F-HiAdm[†]	.255[**]	.000
A-Family[†]	-.041	.478
A-Friends[†]	.007	.900
A-Colleague[†]	-.056	.332
A-LoAdm[†]	-.338[**]	.000
A-HiAdm[†]	-.263[**]	.000
FearJob[†]	-.374[**]	.000
FearPenalty[†]	-.347[**]	.000
Suggest+[†]	-.219[*]	.024
Secrecy[†]	-.051	.370
Hierarchy[†]	-.280[**]	.000
SocDesire[†]	-.243[**]	.000
NoInteract[†]	-.277[**]	.000
BadFeel[†]	-.068	.234
LoMorale[†]	-.175[**]	.002
-WorkQuality[†]	-.199[**]	.000
BadComm[†]	-.123[*]	.031
JobChange[†]	-.293[**]	.000
AdmPractice[†]	-.314[**]	.000
Problem[†]	-.185[**]	.001
Suggestion[†]	-.170[**]	.003
ColegPerform[†]	-.214[**]	.000
Benefits[†]	-.180[**]	.002
Assumptions[†]	-.193[**]	.001
SuggestBox[†]	-.058	.314
RewardVoice[†]	-.020	.727
CompChannel[†]	.017	.771
D-Undiscussable[†]	-.006	.916
JointMeet[†]	-.030	.601
W/Action[†]	-.040	.482

Note.
[**] Correlation is significant at the .01 level.
[*] Correlation is significant at the .05 level.
[†] Please refer to Appendix C for explanations of survey codes.

Table 4.31
College Comparisons as Represented by Mean Values of Different Indexes of Public Secrets[*]

Aspects of public secrets	CofAg	CofAS A	CofB A	C. of Edu.	CofEng	COLA	CMCMA	CofSci	Law School	Med. School
F-Frequency	3.7	3.3	4.5	3.9	4.4	4.2	4.1	3.9	3.6	3.6
F-Family	3.4	3.2	4.2	3.4	4.2	3.6	3.8	3.6	3.5	3.0
F-Friends	3.7	2.7	4.1	3.6	3.9	3.8	3.5	3.3	3.2	3.0
F-Colleague	3.9	3.6	4.6	3.7	4.9	4.2	4.3	3.6	3.3	3.7
F-LoAdm	2.9	1.9	2.7	1.9	2.4	2.2	2.4	2.2	2.5	2.0
F-HiAdm	2.1	1.4	1.6	1.5	1.5	1.7	1.3	1.4	1.9	1.3
A-Family	2.1	1.3	1.6	1.5	1.8	1.8	1.2	1.1	1.1	1.4
A-Friends	1.9	1.4	1.6	1.6	2.1	1.9	1.3	1.1	1.4	1.3
A-Colleague	2.0	1.4	1.8	1.7	1.6	2.0	1.6	1.1	1.6	1.5
A-LoAdm	3.1	3.4	3.9	3.9	4.1	4.1	3.2	2.3	2.2	3.1
A-HiAdm	3.5	3.7	3.9	4.5	4.6	4.3	3.7	2.8	2.6	3.2
FearJob	1.2	2.4	1.8	2.0	1.6	1.9	1.6	1.7	1.6	2.0
FearPenalty	2.1	3.1	2.8	2.6	2.7	2.5	2.8	2.4	2.2	2.7
Suggest+	2.3	2.7	3.2	3.0	3.0	2.8	2.6	2.6	2.4	2.9
Secrecy	1.4	2.4	2.2	2.7	2.1	2.3	2.4	2.0	1.4	1.8
Hierarchy	1.8	2.3	2.3	2.7	2.6	2.7	2.4	2.1	1.7	2.4
SocDesire	2.1	2.3	2.3	2.5	2.4	2.5	2.8	2.0	2.1	2.4
NoInteract	3.1	3.1	3.2	3.3	3.2	3.2	3.0	2.9	2.8	3.2
BadFeel	2.2	1.9	2.0	2.1	2.4	2.4	2.1	2.2	1.2	2.2
LoMorale	1.9	2.2	2.3	2.5	2.6	2.5	2.3	2.4	1.6	2.5
-WorkQuality	1.4	1.7	1.9	2.1	2.1	1.8	1.6	1.7	1.2	2.3
BadComm	2.1	2.8	2.6	2.8	3.1	2.8	2.5	2.8	1.7	2.7
JobChange	1.6	2.0	2.0	2.3	2.2	2.2	1.8	2.3	1.4	2.2
AdmPractice	3.3	3.4	3.9	3.2	4.8	3.6	3.2	2.8	3.3	3.5
Problem	3.0	2.7	3.0	2.8	3.2	3.0	1.6	2.2	1.9	2.4
Suggestion	2.9	2.8	3.0	2.7	3.1	3.1	1.6	2.1	2.0	2.3
ColegPerform	3.2	2.9	3.4	3.0	4.0	3.4	2.8	2.5	2.5	2.9
Benefits	3.1	2.8	3.0	2.9	3.6	3.1	2.0	2.5	1.8	2.3
Assumptions	3.2	3.0	3.4	3.0	3.1	3.3	1.8	2.1	2.0	2.3
SuggestBox	1.9	1.9	1.6	1.6	1.5	1.7	1.9	1.6	1.9	1.5
RewardVoice	2.0	2.2	2.4	2.1	2.3	1.8	2.3	2.2	2.2	1.9
CompChannel	2.1	2.2	2.2	2.1	2.9	2.1	2.3	2.0	2.2	1.9
D-Undiscussable	2.3	2.7	2.6	2.6	2.6	2.4	2.8	2.4	2.9	2.4
JointMeet	2.7	2.3	2.7	2.3	1.8	2.5	2.8	2.6	2.3	2.1
W/Action	3.1	3.2	3.4	3.3	3.3	3.4	3.1	3.1	3.2	3.4

Note.
* Please refer to Appendix C for explanations of survey codes.

To briefly summarize for this section of Chapter Four, female respondents, compared with their male counterparts, tend to be less frank with administrators, have a more concerned perception of the causes of "public secrets," and more frequently avoid certain topics in public/formal discussion. Untenured respondents, compared with their tenured counterparts, tend to be less frank with administrators, have a more concerned perception of the causes of the "public secrets," are more likely to change their jobs in case of dissatisfaction, and more frequently avoid certain topics in public/formal discussion. Respondents with lower salary ranges tend to be less frank with administrators and more impacted by the phenomenon of "public secrets." Finally, respondents with more years of work experience practice "public secrets" slightly less, are slightly more frank with administrators, have a slightly lesser perception of causes of "public secrets," and are slightly more frank with certain topics in public/formal discussion.

5

DISCUSSION

This chapter addresses the implications of the study results in terms of the research questions, questions inspired by relevant literature on the topic, the Web form as a survey tool, suggestions and directions for future research, and conclusion.

RESEARCH QUESTION ONE

RQ1: Does the communication phenomenon of public secrets exist, and, if yes, how widespread is this phenomenon?

As the visual representation of the study results in Figure 5.1 indicates, more than 80% of the respondents express and exchange frank opinions about their institution with family, friends, and colleagues, but not with administrators; nearly 80% of the respondents express and exchange frank opinions about their institution privately, but not publicly—although the frequency of their doing so varied. This shows that the organizational communication phenomenon of public secrets does exist and exists with a compelling potency. Participants' responses to the question, "How often do you express frank opinions about your institution informally, but not formally" (as shown in Table 4.4), confirms this claim.

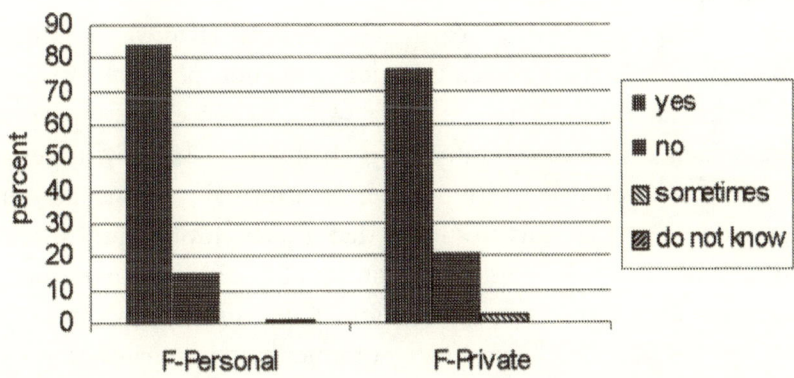

Note.

F-Personal: Do you express and exchange frank opinions about your institution with colleagues, friends, and/or family, but not with administrators?

F-Private: Do you express and exchange frank opinions about your institution privately, but not publicly (e.g., at meetings)?

Figure 5.1
The Phenomenon of Public Secrets is Widespread

Study results (as represented in Table 4.4) also showed that more than 96% of respondents, to varying degrees of frequency, are frank with family, friends, and/or colleagues when expressing opinions about their institution. However, 24.7% of respondents are never frank with low level administration when expressing opinions about their institution and nearly 48% of respondents are only occasionally frank with low level administration. The case with high level administration is more severe: 62% of respondents are never frank with high level administration when expressing opinions about their institution, and 23.7% are only occasionally frank. Study results as summarized in Table 4.5 serve as a confirmation of previous discoveries. No more than 16% of respondents never avoided administrators in their frank expressions about their institution. Results from interviews and comments in the survey also confirm previous findings. All these findings clearly mean that there exists a dichotomy between faculty's communication with personal/informal relationships (family, friends, and colleagues) and their communication with non-personal/formal relationships (administrators). In other words, when expressing opinions about their institution, faculty are generally more frank with personal/ informal relations than with non-personal/formal relations like administration. The necessary result is that much information about the institution in faculty's informal communication is impoverished and absent in their formal communication. This result corroborates my discussion, in Chapter Two, of dichotomies in the organization. More specifically, this result corroborates Kreps and Thornton's (1984) division of organizational communication into informal and formal communications and Stacey's (1996) theory of the legitimate system and the shadow system within the organization.

Yet, how much can be generalized from this study? The present study employed a stratified systematic random method in its selection of subjects and has a sampling size of roughly one third of the subject population. Thus, the respondents are representative of the entire faculty of the subject institution. As a public, comprehensive institution of higher education, the campus is similar to other institutions of similar size and purpose. Thus it is reasonable to conclude that results from the present study are generalizable to other public, comprehensive institutions of higher education in the United States. Therefore, it can be concluded that the communication phenomenon of public secrets exists and does so to a compelling degree in such institutions.

However, since the present study was limited to faculty, no conclusion can yet be generalized to administrative staff or students. Future research needs to expand the generalizability of the study by specifically including administrative staff and students so that the study results would more confidently apply to the entire population body in public, comprehensive institutions of higher education.

Additional research is also needed of other organizations before the findings of the study can be generalized to other organizational types. One could hypothesize that results of the present study are applicable to other types of organizations since tenured faculty at institutions of higher education typically enjoy a greater degree of freedom of expression. Such a hypothesis, however, would need to be tested.

To summarize for research question one, the phenomenon of public secrets exists and does so to a compelling potency in public, comprehensive universities such as the subject institution. Though hypothetically applicable to other types of organizations, the present study needs to acquire expanded generalizability through further research of the entire population body of other types of organizations as well as universities and colleges.

RESEARCH QUESTION TWO

RQ2: What factors do respondents perceive as contributing to the emergence of public secrets?

The survey instrument used for the study suggested seven possible causes of public secrets (FearJob, FearPenalty, Suggest+, Secrecy, Hierarchy, SocDesire, NoInteract; see Appendix C for explanations of the codes). Respondents' perception of the importance of each cause is summarized in Table 4.6. As the results demonstrate, the majority of the respondents perceived that all these suggested causes play a role of varying degrees in contributing to the emergence of public secrets. This shows that the phenomenon of public secrets is certainly multifaceted in its causes. Results from the interviews and comments in the survey even brought up more causes of public secrets. A complete understanding of the causes of public certainly is not a simple task.

Though multifaceted in its causes, the phenomenon of public secrets is not equally explained by each of the causes. Study results demonstrate that some causes have a far greater role than others do in contributing to the emergence of public secrets. In the case of this study, "lack of interaction opportunities with target audience" is by far the most important cause of public secrets. Nearly 85% of respondents think it is either "important" or "very important." In the order of descending importance, what follows "lack of interaction opportunities" are "suggestions unacknowledged with actions," "social desirability," "hierarchy or social stratification," "fear of penalty from administration," "culture of secrecy," and "fear of losing job" which is by far the least important cause of public secrets.

The finding that different factors have very varied degrees of importance in contributing to the emergence of public secrets offers valuable information for future research. It implies that different causes of public secrets should be approached differently and with different amounts of attention. It also implies that different strategies to alleviate public secrets are of varied effectiveness because of the correlation between the potency of solutions and the correct analysis of causes. For instance, in the case of the subject organization in this study, strategies that promise to increase interaction between faculty and administration will probably be effective in alleviating public secrets.

Because of the fact that modern organizations have a variety of structures and purposes, the same set of causes of public secrets may not be applicable to every type of organization. Additional research is necessary to determine the specific set of causes of public secrets in each type of organization. Even each organization needs to study the unique set of causes of public secrets within its own boundaries. For instance, since tenure plays an important role in affording job security for faculty, "fear of losing job" turned out to be a not so significant factor in the emergence of public secrets in the case of the subject organization in this study. The situation can be vastly different in other types of organizations where employees do not hold tenure.

In short, the suggested causes were confirmed as playing roles of different degrees in contributing to the emergence of public secrets. Public secrets are multifaceted and varied in their causes, and the study of such causes in different organizations should be approached differently.

RESEARCH QUESTION THREE

RQ3: What do respondents perceive as the impact of public secrets on organizational health and organizational members' quality of work?

As study results summarized in Table 4.7 demonstrate, bad communication climate emerged as the most severe negative consequence from an organizational culture that contains a high level of public secrets. This clearly shows a strong correlation between public secrets and a negative communication climate. Yet the present study did not include an investigation of the nature of this correlation. Does the phenomenon of public secrets lead to a negative communication climate? Or does a negative communication climate lead to public secrets? Or are they mutually reproductive, making the relationship one like that between chicken and egg? These questions were not included in the agenda of the present study and wait for future investigation. Further research is justified because of the common belief that a clear understanding of relationships effectively contributes to the discovery of solutions.

Hypothetically, the pre-existence of a negative communication climate is the fertile soil for the weeds of public secrets, and after that, the relationship between the two becomes a mutually reproductive one. People are simply not born with the habit of choosing to speak differently in different contexts. Children's simple frankness, regardless of situation and people, serves as a proof (the kid in the story of "the King's New Clothes" is a pertinent example). People learn to practice public secrets through what they experience in their environment.

After the existence of public secrets is established, the relationship between public secrets and a negative communication climate is probably changed into a mutually reproductive one. That is, public secrets both result from and produce a negative climate of organizational communication. Public secrets signal to people that some information or topics are expressible only in restrained contexts within the organization. Under the influence of this signal, organizational members tend to become further restrained in their expression of information and knowledge concerning their organization, which, in turn, produces more public secrets. A vicious cycle develops between public secrets and a negative communication climate. Yet this speculation requires research to be verified.

Study results as summarized in Table 4.7 also demonstrate that "negative impact on quality of work" turned out to be the least severe consequence from the phenomenon of public secrets. That is, a climate of public secrets does not seem to exert as an important impact upon faculty's teaching and research which accounts for the bulk for their work. Fortunately, explanations for this finding are already obtainable from comments in the survey. One comment in the survey reported, "As a teacher, it is entirely possible (and often necessary) to separate one's students from [the institution] as a whole, so that 'quality of work' when it comes to teaching may not necessarily suffer because we recognize that the students do not deserve to be neglected." This is understandable because of the special nature of the teaching profession and the sense of nobility from the "engineers of human souls" (teachers).

Yet is this interpretation applicable to "engineers" of other things, those of industrial products, for example, where a lesser sense of responsibility is perhaps necessitated? That is, do public secrets also exert comparatively the least impact on quality of work in types of organizations different from universities and colleges? This question points to another need for future research.

Although the negative impact from public secrets is comparatively less obvious on professors' teaching and research, this impact does get manifested in many other things that include a low morale, contemplation of job transfer, and negative feelings about the organization. This finding reveals that the "curse" of public secrets is not simple but varied and multifaceted. This finding helps to further justify the significance of the present study and continued studies of public secrets in the future.

To recapitulate, the phenomenon of public secrets is varied and multifaceted in its negative consequences as it is in its causes. In the case of the present study, "bad communication climate" is the most severe consequence and "negative impact on quality of work" is the least severe consequence from public secrets. The specific nature of the relationship between public secrets and a bad communication climate awaits more research.

RESEARCH QUESTION FOUR

RQ4: In what areas do public secrets exist?

Six areas (AdmPractice, Problem, Suggestion, ColegPerform, Benefits, and Assumptions; see Appendix C for explanations of survey codes) were suggested as topics that may be avoided in public/formal discussion. Results from the study affirm that the vast majority of respondents avoid formal/public discussion of these topics at least "occasionally." This clearly demonstrates that there do exist various areas or topics that are avoided in public/formal discussion. Such topics point toward the areas in which an organization needs to improve its communication by alleviating the public secrets in these areas.

Among the six suggested topics, "colleague performance" appears to be the most salient one. This may mean that collegiality is a much espoused value in the setting of a university. Collegiality is an easy reminder of one of the most important causes of public secrets, social desirability. Obviously, criticizing one's colleagues is not defined as "socially desirable." Public secrets, in turn, acquire a cultural dimension since what is socially desirable and what is not is generally a cultural phenomenon and definition. Study of public secrets necessarily involves the study of culture, especially those cultural elements that address social desirability, ethics, and taboos. Alleviation of public secrets necessitates modifications and alterations to the culture, making the task a formidable one. All this shows a direction where future investigation may invest its efforts.

As mentioned previously, study findings also affirmed other suggested topics besides colleague performance as topics avoided in public/formal discussion. These topics include administrative practices, problems, suggestions, assumptions, and compensation and benefits. These affirmed topics help define strategies to alleviate public secrets. If organizational members are afraid of publicly or formally addressing administrative practices and problems in the organization, the administrators in that organization need to modify their governance philosophy and leadership style. If organizational members avoid public/formal presentation and discussion of suggestions, accepted assumptions, and compensation and benefits, administrators may need to endeavor to reframe the climate of their organizational communication so that more openness is introduced and less defensiveness is involved. This leads to the discussion of research question five, strategies to alleviate public secrets.

RESEARCH QUESTION FIVE

RQ5: Are the suggested strategies to allay the phenomenon of public secrets effective in respondents' perception?

Six strategies (SuggestBox, RewardVoice, CompChannel, D-Undiscussable, JointMeet, and W/Action; see Appendix C for explanations of survey codes) were suggested to solicit the respondents' perception of the effectiveness of these strategies to alleviate the phenomenon of public secrets. There was a drastic contrast between "suggestion box" and "acknowledging suggestions with actions." Among the six suggested strategies, "suggestion box" is by far the least effective, and "acknowledging suggestions with actions" is by far the most effective. This obviously demonstrates people's weariness about mere talk and their yearning for actions on the part of administration. Many interviewees and commentators to the survey expressed their pessimism about the effectiveness of "suggestion box" as a strategy to alleviate the phenomenon of public secrets. Words without actions, as they reported, are really weary and dreary. This points a need for administrators to have a greater appreciation of Kouzes and Posner's (1993) concept of leadership credibility, which is achieved more through deeds than through words.

Since there is a close logical connection between causes of a problem and strategies to solve the problem, survey results about possible causes of public secrets promise to offer inspiration about strategies to alleviate public secrets. In respondents' perception, the most important cause of public secrets is lack of interaction opportunities with administration. This input illustrates an invaluable direction for future research for strategies to alleviate public secrets. That is, mechanisms that increase interaction opportunities between organizational members and administrators/managers hold promise to alleviate public secrets. Hypothetically, such mechanisms or strategies may include, for example, administrators' personal visits to grassroots departments within the organization, regular meetings between administration and faculty, direct electronic connection between the administration and frontline organizational members, and the leaning of the bureaucratic body within the organization so that the social distance between administration and organizational members is shortened. Other strategies to alleviate public secrets, as suggested in a panel discussion about shared governance, include publication outlets for information that administration does not like. These publication outlets may include union newsletter, local newspaper, and radio and TV stations. The whole spectrum of possible strategies and the effectiveness of the previously mentioned strategies await further investigation.

Search for strategies to alleviate public secrets may be one of the ultimate purposes of the research about public secrets. Research about the causes, consequences, and topics concerning public secrets should all be given attention by future research of public secrets because research about all these factors contributes to discovery of effective strategies to transform sharable knowledge in public secrets into actable knowledge to guide organizational actions.

DISCUSSION OF GROUP DIFFERENCES AND CORRELATIONS

As survey results presented in Chapter Four demonstrate, concerning the general practice of "public secrets," there is no significant difference between various groups of respondents in terms of their sex, tenure, and salary range. No significant difference was found either among different colleges of the subject institution concerning their practice of "public secrets." This illustrates that "public secrets" represent a phenomenon in which different categories or groups of organizational members participate, giving more ubiquity to this communication phenomenon. And because of this ubiquity, the phenomenon of "public secrets" compels serious attention.

Also as discernible from the survey results, female respondents, compared with their male counterparts, tend to be less frank with administrators, have a more concerned perception of the causes of "public secrets," and more frequently avoid certain topics in public/formal discussion. These differences between male and female respondents do not lend themselves to an easy explanation. It is perhaps because administrators are more often men than women, thus making the general interaction between administrators and women more difficult than that between administrators and men. Perhaps women have a stronger sense of social appropriateness in terms of public/formal expression than men do, and therefore are more restrained in public/formal expression. Perhaps women are more concerned than are men about the communication climate in their organization, leading women to have a more concerned perception of the causes of "public secrets." Since these questions were not included in the agenda of the present study, they are not answered by findings of this study. They do, however, provide directions for future research. An effort to seek answers to these questions is necessary because study of differences between groups that practice "public secrets" differently will better our understanding of the causes of "public secrets," and thus better the chances of finding more effective strategies to alleviate "public secrets" in the organizational setting.

Respondents with tenure and with more years of work experience were slightly more frank in their public/formal expression, less restrained in their interaction with administrators, and less concerned about losing their jobs. This is not hard to comprehend with the consideration that these respondents enjoy greater protection through their tenure and probably feel more "at home" with their organization because of their longer years of work experience. This finding offers a clear implication that more security on the part of organizational members will help free up their expression and help alleviate the phenomenon of "public secrets." The original rationale behind the concept of tenure is exactly so.

Respondents with a higher salary range are either tenured faculty or, if not tenured, faculty in a highly marketable field. Thus, they are also protected, either through tenure or through the marketability of their field. As a result, these respondents also seem more frank in their public/formal expression. In short, a greater sense of protection on the part of organizational members appears to help alleviate the phenomenon of "public secrets" and free up expression.

IMPLICATIONS AND QUESTIONS INSPIRED BY RELEVANT LITERATURE

Results from the present study reveal that regarding information and knowledge concerning their organization, faculty's informal communication with more personal relations and their formal communication with administration are not always compatible. The level of the latter obviously falls behind that of the former. Faculty members also more frequently avoid communication with administration than they do with their more personal relations (family, friends, and colleagues). The necessary result is a discrepancy between communications in different contexts and a likely rift between faculty and administration. Such discrepancy and rift indicate a non-systemic functioning of the organization as explained in the literature on systems theory. In other words, the phenomenon of public secrets signals a non-systemically functioning organization in that, as results of the present study have shown, public secrets contain a non-compatibility of communications in different contexts.

As explained in Chapter Two, Stacey (1996) contends that an innovative organization operates "at the edge of chaos" where the shadow system (or informal communication system in Kreps and Thorton's [1984] words) confronts, invades, and undermines the legitimate system (or formal communication system, again in Kreps and Thorton's words). Results about the subject organization in the present study show a different picture that deviates from Stacey's image of the innovative organization. Public secrets emerge in the subject organization not because of "confrontation, invasion, or undermining," but because of retreating and avoiding. Organizational members retreat in their formal/public communication and avoid formal/public discussion of certain topics either because of their fear of or because of their lack of interaction opportunities with the administration. Thus public secrets do not herald an innovative but a stagnant organization.

Also as shown in the study results, the phenomenon of public secrets involves fear and defense. According to Gibb (1961), fear and defense lead to a defensive communication climate, which, in turn, tends to breed information/communication distortion. The necessary inference is that the phenomenon of public secrets tends to breed defensive communication and information distortion. According to the literature on organizational learning, gathering of genuine and accurate information plays a defining role in a learning organization. Thus, the phenomenon of public secrets is not congruent with the concept of the learning organization. This again illustrates why public secrets signal a stagnant and non-innovative organization as mentioned previously.

As also explained in Chapter Two, there is a correlation between organizational communication and organizational members' morale. Results for this study confirm this contention. More than 80% of the respondents perceive that an organizational culture containing a high level of public secrets leads to low morale of different degrees. Nearly 80% of the respondents believe that there is a connection between public secrets and contemplation of job relocation, which surely is a signal of low morale. To liberate organizational members from the restraining experience caused by public secrets, taboos need to be broken. This is also confirmed by the study results. First, more than 80% of the respondents avoid the suggested topics at least occasionally in public/formal settings. Second, more than half of the respondents believe that, to alleviate public secrets, it is an effective strategy to discuss "undiscussables" or taboos, especially when this discussion is initiated by administration. Therefore, there seems to exist a sequential relationship here: overcoming taboos → alleviation of public secrets → better communication climate → higher morale and better organizational learning → better health for the organization.

THE WEB FORM AS A SURVEY TOOL

This study used a Web-based survey. Several revelations from experimenting with the Web as a means for collecting data may prove helpful for future research. Both advantages and disadvantages were found in using the Web form as a survey tool. Previously hypothesized, many of these advantages and disadvantages were confirmed by results from this study.

First, the Web form provides better anonymity for the respondents. Responses sent through a Web Form Monitor will completely block the e-mail address and identification of the sender. E-mail addresses sent through the "bcc" function will also completely conceal these addresses from the receivers of the message. Consequently, survey participants do not know who among their colleagues or acquaintances are also included in the survey population and thus more likely feel a better psychological safety and ease in answering the questionnaire and providing further comments. This point was affirmed by some comments in the survey.

Second, the Web form makes verbal comments much easier for the respondents. To the vast majority of people, writing through the keyboard is much more facile than with the hand. Thus the Web form offer a better promise in soliciting respondents' comments. One survey respondent commented, "This is an interesting on-line survey experience. You set it up nicely and it is easy to complete." Different from a paper survey instrument, an on-line survey entails no length restriction on comments. Facilitated by this advantage, some comments to the survey were as long as twenty printed lines. Thus, an on-line survey promises a better compensation for the restraining standardized format of the survey instrument.

Third, the Web survey is more economical and expeditious. Without the necessity of printing out copies of the survey instrument and sending them to potential respondents through postal mail as in the case of a paper survey instrument, the financial cost for the survey of this study neared zero, although my cost in time designing the Web form skyrocketed. Also, electronic responses are obviously much quicker than what gets through the postal mail which is nicknamed the "snail mail" in our age of electronic mail. The majority of the responses to the survey of this study were received within two weeks after the cover letter was sent out.

Fourth, in terms of data entry, an on-line survey is a great contributor to data accuracy. Responses sent to the researcher's e-mail box are electronically stored and can be automatically transported into a survey software like SPSS. This will drastically help decrease data error that may be caused by manual entry.

Fifth, the major difficulty involved in an on-line survey lies in the process of collecting potential respondents' e-mail addresses and in the necessary technicality involved in electronic administration of the survey. It is not always easy to acquire people's e-mail addresses. My situation was less complicated since the subject institution has its own on-line directories and the subject population involved only one location. Despite this fact, I spent almost ten days gleaning faculty's e-mail addresses from the on-line directories of different departments. This process of collecting e-mail addresses poses another problem. The researcher may end up sending the survey to people who are not part of the desired population. If a department's on-line directory is not updated, it may contain defunct e-mail addresses, addresses of people who have stopped working at the subject organization, and addresses of people who have changed their e-mail addresses. The necessary technicality involved in an on-line survey can also pose a problem. Respondents may quit their effort in responding to the survey because of slow entry into the website of the survey or slow down-loading of the survey questionnaire. When I sent my survey the second time to the subject population, about 60 people responded to me that they could not open the survey web-page by clicking the provided link. As a result, I had to respond to every one of these people, suggesting that, instead of directly clicking the link, they copy and paste the link into the address bar of their web browser. I do not know how many respondents were pushed away by this inconvenience since I received quite a few complaints from some respondents about this inconvenience.

Finally, the major risk of an on-line survey is its potentially low response rate. Different from an on-spot administration of a paper survey instrument, receivers of an on-line survey feel a much less obligation to respond. Since the researcher does not know the identification of the respondent, the researcher finds it hard to track those who have not responded to the survey. Consequently, in an effort to increase the response rate, the researcher has to send the survey a second time, and even a third time, to the same participants. This may be perceived by many participants (especially those who have responded) as "spam" or junk mail. A resulting unpleasant feeling may cause the subjects to deliberately refuse to respond to the questionnaire if they have not responded to the survey in the first place. I must say that I am very lucky in having a response rate of over 60% in the case of this study.

The advantages of an on-line survey obviously outweigh its disadvantages. With rapid development of technology, the Web form will acquire more prominence as a survey tool. Further investigation of this survey tool will surely help discovery of better research methods.

LIMITATIONS OF THIS STUDY AND SUGGESTIONS AND DIRECTIONS FOR FUTURE RESEARCH

One major difficulty that is encountered in this study is the measurement of how often people avoid doing something. Three interviewees and some commentators to the survey reported that they had difficulty in indicating the frequency of their avoiding communication with administration, despite the fact that a definition of avoidance was given. These respondents did not perceive the act of avoiding as an act. For future research, more understandable measurement concepts and components need to be designed to measure the act of avoiding. In view of lack of established survey tools for the topic of this study, more accurate and developed survey instruments need to be designed for future research on public secrets.

Since the frequency of communicative behavior is not amenable to easy measurement, measurement of the severity of public secrets through frequency of communicative behavior may not be the ideal method. How to measure the severity of the phenomenon of public secrets poses another question for future research.

Subject population for this study comes from one type of organization, a public institution of higher education. The range of applicability of the results of this study waits for the verification by further investigation of other types of organizations. Tenure, as one distinctive feature in institutions of higher education, for instance, may make universities and colleges very different from other types of organizations. The stated convention of shared governance, as another distinctive feature, may create an expectation of more input from faculty members.

Public secrets, as a communication phenomenon, occur not only in organizational communication. This phenomenon may exist in various other settings such intercultural communication, family communication, political communication, mass communication, and religious communication. Thus study of the phenomenon of public secrets may be broadened beyond the organizational setting into other types of settings of human communication. In short, due to lack of established research on the topic of public secrets, the present study may serve more as an invitation than as a revelation.

CONCLUSION

The phenomenon of public secrets is theoretically founded and empirically proved. Results from this study offer bits of new knowledge on the phenomenon of public secrets as well as serve as a confirmation of many contentions in pertinent research literature.

As demonstrated by the study results, the phenomenon of public secrets does exist and exists with compelling severity, at least in the case of the subject organization of this study. Organizational members generally have a higher degree of frank expression in their informal communication with more personal relations than in their formal communication with administration. Among the causes of public secrets, lack of interaction with administration turned out to be the most important. The second most important cause is that organizational members' suggestions and input are not acknowledged with administrative actions. Among the negative consequences from public secrets, bad communication climate and low morale are the most serious ones. Contemplation of job change follows these two as the next most serious consequence. According to Rusbult's (1987) communication theory, contemplation of job change may be interpreted as the "exit" style of conflict solution, which is actively destructive to the involved relationship.

Public secrets are manifested in various topics which organizational members tend to avoid in public/formal discussion. In the case of this study, colleague performance and administrative practices are among the top topics that tend to be avoided in public/formal discussion. As conventional wisdom may anticipate, acknowledging organizational members' input with actions turned out to be the most effective strategy to alleviate public secrets in the respondents' perception. Deliberate effort to overcome "undiscussables" or taboos on the part of administration turned out to be the next most effective strategy. These perceptions of respondents may represent their wish for more credibility, honesty, and trust on the part of administration.

Also as indicated by the study results, there does exist, in organizational communication, a dichotomy between formal and informal communication or between the shadow system and the legitimate system. Organizational members' tacit knowledge is more manifested in their informal communication because of their higher frequency of communication in this communication. Systemic functioning of the organization requires a collaborative co-existence between the formal and informal communications within the organization. Otherwise the organization wastes a rich knowledge repository that lies in its shadow system. The phenomenon of public secrets involves taboos that tend to breed defensive communication, which in turn tends to breed information/communication distortion. For better organizational health and employee motivation, the organization must learn to overcome taboos and public secrets. Harmony within the organizational communication will help produce harmony in the organizational members' work and life.

Because of the myriad of restrictions upon human communicational behavior, more may be communicated in non-communication than in communication. The study of the oxymoron of public secrets confronts the intersecting intersection point between communication and non-communication and thus promises to be more fruitful than study of only manifested communication. I hope that the study of public secrets will blaze a new and refreshing trail in the field of communication studies, and that fruits from this effort will help make the garden of human life a better place to dwell in.

REFERENCES

Alexander, M. J. (1974). <u>Information systems analysis</u>. Chicago: Science Research Associates.

Argyris, C. (1973). <u>On organizations of the future</u>. Beverly Hills, CA: Sage.

Argyris, C. (1990). <u>Overcoming organizational defense</u>. Needham, MA: Allyn and Bacon.

Argyris, C. (1991). Teaching smart people how to learn. <u>Harvard Business Review, 69</u>, 99–109.

Argyris, C., & Schön, D. (1978). <u>Organizational learning: A theory of action perspective.</u> Reading, MA: Addison-Wesley.

Argyris, C. & Schön, D. A. (1996). <u>Organizational learning II: Theory, method, and practice</u>. Reading, MA: Addison-Wesley.

Arnold, W. W. & Plas, J.M. (1993). <u>The human touch: Today's most unusual program for productivity and profit</u>. New York: John Wiley & Sons, Inc.

Athanassiades, J. C. (1973). The distortion of upward communication in hierarchical organizations. <u>Academy of Management Journal, 16</u>, 207–226.

Babbie, E. (1990). <u>Survey research methods</u> (2nd ed.). Belmont, CA: Wadsworth.

Barnard, C. I. (1938). The function of the executive. Cambridge, MA: Harvard.

Bennis, W. (1976). The unconscious conspiracy: Why leaders can't lead. New York: American Management Association.

Bennis, W. (1989). Why leaders can't lead: The unconscious conspiracy continues. San Francisco: Jossey-Bass.

Bennis, W. & Nanus, B. (1985). Leaders: The strategies for taking charge. New York: Haper & Row.

Bertalanffy, L. (1951). General system theory: A new approach to the unity of science. Human Biology, Decemeber, 1951, 303–361.

Bertalanffy, L. (1952). Problems of life: An evaluation of modern biological thought. New York: Wiley.

Bertalanffy, L. (1968). General system theory. New York: George Braziller.

Bertalanffy, L. (1975). Perspectives on general systems theory: Scientific-philosophical studies. New York: George Braziller.

Bertalanffy, L. (1981). A systems view of man. Boulder, CO: Westview.

Bok, S. (1978). Lying: Moral choice in public and private life. New York: Random House.

Bomm, D. R., Blakeney, R. N., & Matteson, M. R. (Eds.). (1973). The individual and the organization. New York: Harper & Row.

Bresser, R. K. & Bishop, R. C. (1983). Dysfunctional effect of formal planning. Academy of Management, 8, 588–599.

Browne, R. B. (Ed.).(1984). Forbidden Fruits: Taboos and tabooism in culture. Bowling Green, Ohio: Bowling Green University Popular Press.

Burke, K. (1990). Language as symbolic action. In P. Bizzel & B. Herzberg (Eds.), The rhetorical tradition: Readings from classical times to the present (pp. 1034–1041). Boston: St. Martin's.

Butterfield, F. (1990). China: Alive in the bitter sea. New York: Times Books.

Capozzoli, T. K. (1997). Creating a motivating environment for employees. Supervision, 58, 16–18.

Carley, K. M. & Lin, Z. (1997). A theoretical study of organizational performance under information distortion. Management Science, 43, 976–997.

Castaneda, C. (1971). A separate reality. New York: Simon & Schuster.

Chase, A. B. (1970). How to make downward communication work. Personnel Journal, 49, 478–483.

Cohen, D. (1997). Managing knowledge for business success: A conference report. New York: Conference Board.

Covey, S. R. (1989). The seven habits of highly effective people: Restoring the character ethic. New York: Simon and Schuster.

Covey, S. R. (1991). Principle-centered leadership. New York: Summit Books.

Covey, S. R. (1993a). How to succeed with people. Salt Lake City, UT: Deseret Book Co.

Covey, S. R. (1993b). Spiritual roots of human relations. Salt Lake City, Utah: Deseret Book.

Covey, S. R. (1994). First things first: To live, to love, to learn, to leave a legacy. New York: Simon & Schuster.

Crampton, S. M., Hodge, J. W., & Mishra, J. M. (1998). The informal communication network: Factors influencing grapevine activity. Public Personnel Management, 27, 569–584.

Davis, K. (1973). The organization that's not on the chart. In R. C. Huseman, C. M. Logue, & D. L. Freshley (Eds.), Readings in interpersonal and organizational communication (pp. 149–154). Boston: Holbrook Press.

Davis, T. R. V. (1996). Developing an employee balanced scorecard: Linking frontline performance to corporate objectives. Frontline Associates Marketing, 101, 17.

Davis, W. & O'Conner, J. R. (1977). Serial transmission of information: A study of the grapevine. Journal of Applied Communication Research, 5, 61–72.

Deagal, S. & Horne, D. (1997). Human dynamics: A new framework for understanding people and realizing the potential in our organizations. Cambridge, MA: Pegasus Communications.

Deming, W. E. (1986). Out of the crisis. Cambridge, MA: Center for Advanced Engineering Study (MIT).

Deming, W. E. (1993). The new economics. Cambridge, MA: Center for Advanced Engineering Study (MIT).

Dettmer, H. W. (1998). Breaking the Constraints to World-Class Performance, Milwaukee, WI: ASQ Quality Press.

Dewar, D. L. (1980). The quality circle guide to participative management. Englewood Cliffs, NJ: Prentice-Hall.

Dewey, J. (1938). Logic: The theory of inquiry. New York: Holt, Rinehart and Winston.

Deutsch, A. (1979). The human resources revolution: Communicate or litigate. New York: McGraw-Hill.

Dormann, H. O. (Ed.). (1987). The speaker's book of quotations. New York: Ballantine Books.

Downs, A. (1967). Inside bureaucracy. Boston: Little Brown.

Downs, C. W. & Hain, T. (1982). Productivity and communication. In M. Burgoon (Ed.), Communication Yearbook, 5 (pp. 435–453). New Brunswick, NJ: Transaction Books.

Drucker, P. F. (1986). The frontiers of management: Where tomorrow's decisions are being shaped today. New York: Harper & Row.

Drucker, P. F. (1988). "The coming of the new organization." Harvard Business Review, January-February, p. 47.

Drucker, P. F. (1993). Post-capitalist society. Oxford: Butterworth Heinemann.

Espejo, R. (1994). What is systemic thinking? Systems Dynamics Review, 10, 199–212.

Estes, R. (1996). Tyranny of the bottom line: Why corporations make good people do bad things. San Francisco: Berrett-Koehler.

Feng, D. S. (1998). Dazhai in the eyes of reporters. Today's Celebrity [On-line], 4. Available: http://www.xys.org/xys/ebooks/others/history/contemporary/Dazai.txt

Fisher, D. (1981). Communication in organizations. St. Paul, MN: West Publishing.

Fletcher, J. L. (1993). Patterns of high performance: Discovering the ways people work best. San Francisco: Berrett-Koehler.

Follett, M. P. (1940). The giving of orders. In H. C. Metcalf & L. Urwick (Eds.), Dynamic administration: The collected papers of Mary Parker Follett (pp. 50–70). New York: Harper & Brothers.

Follett, M. P. (1971). The giving of orders. In D. S. Pugh (Ed.), Organization theory. New York: Penguin.

Frohman, M. A. (1996). Unleash urgency and action. Industry Week, 245, 13–15.

Fulk, J. (1986). Distortion in communication in hierarchical relationships. In M. McLaughlin (Ed.), Communication Yearbook, 9, 483–507.

Galbraith, J. (1973). Designing complex organizations. Menlo Park, CA: Addison-Wesley.

Galbraith, J. (1977). Organization design. Reading, MA: Addison-Wesley.

Gehani, R. (May 1994). The tortoise vs. the hare. Quality Progress, 27, 99–103.

Gibb, J. R. (1961). Defensive communication. Journal of Communication, 11, 141–48.

Gibb, J. R. (1978). Trust: A new view of personal and organizational development. Los Angeles, CA: Guild of Tutors Press.

Gordon, M. E. (1984). Grievances: A review of the literature. Personnel Psychology, 37, 117–146.

Haasen, A. & Shea, G.F. (1997). A better place to work: A new sense of motivation leading to high productivity. New York: American Management Association.

Hackney, R. (1999). Strategic information systems planning: Perspectives on the role of the "end-user" revisited. Journal of End User Computing, 11, 3–12.

Haney, W. (1972). Communication and organizational behavior: Text and cases. Homewood, IL: Irwin.

Harris, J. (1996). Getting employees to fall in love with your company. New York: American Management Association.

Harrison, T. M. (1994). Communication and interdependence in "democratic organizations." In S. Deetz (Ed.), Communication Yearbook, 17 (pp. 247–274). Thousand Oaks, CA: Sage.

Helgesen, S. (1995). The web of inclusion. New York: Doubleday.

Heron, A. R. (1942). Sharing information with employees. Stanford, CA: Stanford University Press.

Herzberg, F. (1968). One more time: How do you motivate employees? Harvard Business Review, 46, 53–62.

Herzberg, F. (1973). Work and the nature of man. New York: World Publishing.

Herzberg, F., Mausner, B., & Snyderman, B. B. (1992). The motivation to work. New Brunswick, NJ: Transactions.

Hesselbein, F., Goldsmith, M., & Beckhard, R. (Eds.). (1996). The leader of the future. San Francisco: Jossey-Bass.

Hesselbein, F., Goldsmith, M., & Beckhard, R. (Eds.). (1997). The organization of the future. San Francisco: Jossey-Bass.

Hunt, J. T. (198). Communication skills in the organization. Englewood Cliffs, NJ: Prentice-Hall.

Issacs, W. (1993). Dialogue: The power of collective thinking. The Systems Thinker, 4 (No. 3), pp.1–4.

Janis, I. (1967). Victims of groupthink: A psychological study of foreign decisions and fiascos. Boston: Houghton Mifflin.

Jensen, T. & Bryant, J. (1993). Cooperation, not confrontation, solves sanitation problems. Public Works, 124, 35–37.

Joinson, C. (1996). Re-creating the indifferent employee. HRMagazine, 41, 76–80.

Karathanos, P. & Auriemmo, A. (1999). Care and feeding of the organizational grapevine. Industrial Management, 41, 26–30.

Kilman, R. H., Kilman, I., & Associates. (1994). Managing ego energy: The transformation of personal meaning into organizational success. San Francisco: Jossey-Bass.

Knight, K. & McDaniel, R. (1979). Organizations: An information systems perspective. Belmont, CA: Wadsworth.

Kouzes, J. M. & Posner, B. Z. (1993). Credibility: How leaders gain and lose it, why people demand it. San Francisco: Jossey-Bass.

Kreps, G. L. & Thornton, B. C. (1984). Health communication: Theory and practice. White Plains, NY: Longman.

Krivonos, P. D. (1978). The relationship of intrinsic-extrinsic motivation and communication climate in organizations. Journal of Business Communications, 15, 53–65.

Landsberg, M. (1996). The tao of coaching: Boost your effectiveness at work by inspiring and developing those around you. London: Harper Collins Publishers.

Larkin, T. J. & Larkin, S. (1996). Reaching and changing frontline employees. Harvard Business Review, 4, 95–104.

Lawler III, E.E. (1973). Motivation in work organizations. Monterey, CA: Brooks/Cole Publishing Company.

Lawrence, P. & Lorsch, J. W. (1969). Developing organizations: Diagnosis and action. Reading, MA: Addison-Wesley.

Lehere, R.N. (1982). Participative productivity and quality of work life. Englewood Cliffs, NJ: Prentice-Hall.

Likert, R. (1961). New patterns of management. New York: McGraw-Hill.

Liu, A. P. L. (1986). How China is ruled. Englewood Cliffs, NJ: Prentice-Hall.

Liu, B. (1990). China's crisis, China's hope. Cambridge, MA: Harvard University Press.

Lorey, W. (1980). Mutual trust is the key to open communication. Administrative Management, 37, 70–72, 74, 92.

Malin, M. H. (1983). Protecting the whistle-blower from retaliatory discharge. University of Michigan Journal of Law Reform, 16, 277–318.

Maslow, A. H. (1954). Motivation and Personality. New York: Harper & Row.

Maslow, A. H. (1968). Toward a psychology of being. (2nd ed.). New York: Van Nostrand Reinhold Company.

Maynard, R. (1996). A less-stressed workforce. Nation's Business, 84, 50–51.

Mayo, E. (1933). The human problems of industrial civilization. New York: Macmillan.

McGill, M. E., Slocum, J. W., & Lei, D. (1992). Management practices in learning organizations. Organizational Dynamics, 22, 5–17.

McGregor, D. (1960). The human side of enterprise. New York: McGraw-Hill.

McLuhan, M. (1964). Understanding media: The extensions of man. New York: McGraw-Hill.

McNerney, D. J. (1996). Creating a motivated workforce. HR-Focus, 73, 1–4.

Mehrabian, A. & Ferris, S. R. (1967). Inference of attitudes from nonverbal communication in two channels. Journal of Consulting Psychology, 31, 248–52.

Meyer, A. (1981). How ideologies supplant formal structures and shape responses to environments. Journal of Management Studies, 19, 45–61.

Meyer, H. M., Kay, E., & French, J. R. P. (1965). Split roles in performance appraisals. Harvard Business Review, 43, 123–29.

Miceli, M. P. & Near, J. P. (1984). The relationships among beliefs, organizational position, and whistle-blowing status: A discriminant analysis. Academy of Management Journal, 27, 687–705.

Miceli, M. P. & Near, J. P. (1992). Blowing the whistle: The organizational and legal implications for companies and employees. New York: Lexington Books.

Mumby, D. K. (1984). Ideology and power in organization. Unpublished doctoral dissertation, Southern Illinois University.

Nader, R., Petkas, P. J., & Blackwell, K. (Eds.). (1972). Whistle blowing: The report of the conference on professional responsibility. New York: Grossman.

Near, J. P. & Jenson, T. C. (1983). The whistle blowing process: retaliation and perceived effectiveness. Work and Occupations, 10, 3–28.

Nietzsche, F. (1990). On truth and lies in a nonmoral sense. In P. Bizzel & B. Herzberg (Eds.), The rhetorical tradition: Readings from classical times to the present (pp. 888–896). Boston: St. Martin's.

Nonaka, I. & Takeuchi, H. (1995). The knowledge-creating company. New York: Oxford University Press.

Norman, A. L. (1993). Informational society: An economic theory of discovery, invention and innovation. Boston: Kluwer Academic Publishers.

Ottaway, R. N. (1979). Change agents at work. London: Associated Business.

O'Toole, J. (1996). Leading change: The argument for values-based leadership. San Francisco: Jossey-Bass.

Pan, J. K. (1999). Why "angels in white" go against their obligation? China New Digest [On-line], 430. Available: http://www.cnd.org/HXWZ/CM99/cm9906d.hz8.html

Peters, C. & Branch, T. (1972). Blowing the whistle: dissent in the public' interest. New York: Praeger.

Peters, T. J. & Waterman, R. H. (1982). In search of excellence: Lessons from America's best-run companies. New York: Harper & Row.

Pinder, C.C. (1998). Work motivation in organizational behavior. Upper Saddle River, NJ: Prentice-Hall.

Postrel, V. (1999). The bonds of life. Reason, 30, 22–34.

Redding, W. C. (1984). The corporate manager's guide to better communication. Glenview, IL: Scott, Foresman.

Roberts, K. H. & O'Reilly, C. A. (1974). Failure in upward communication in organizations: Three possible culprits. Academy of Management Journal, 17, 205–215.

Rodeghier, M. (1996). Surveys with confidence. Chicago: SPSS Inc.

Ross, W. D. (1966). Business in a free society. Columbus, OH: Charles E. Merrill Books.

Rost, J. C. (1993). Leadership for the twenty-first century. Westport, CT: Praeger.

Roy, D. F. (1960). Banana time: Job satisfaction and informal interaction. Human Organization, 18, 156–168.

Ruldoph, E. E. (1973). Informal human communication systems in a large organization. Journal of Applied Communication Research, 1, 7–23.

Rusbult, C. E. (1987). Responses to dissatisfaction in close relationships: The exit-voice-loyalty-neglect model. In D. Perlman & S. W. Duck (Eds.), Intimate relationships: Development, dynamics, and deterioration (pp. 109–238). London: Sage.

Ryan, K. D. & Oestreich, D. K. (1991). Driving fear out of the work-place: How to overcome the invisible barriers to quality, productivity, and innovation. San Francisco: Jossey-Bass.

Schein, E. H. (1992). Organizational culture and leadership (2nd ed.). San Francisco: Jossey-Bass.

Schein, E. H. (1993). On dialogue, culture and organizational learning. Organizational Dynamics, 22, 40–51.

Sefton, L. (1999). Does increased employee participation affect job satisfaction, communication satisfaction, and organizational commitment? A quantitative study incorporating the views of both management and non-management. Unpublished dissertation. Southern Illinois University at Carbondale.

Senge, P. M. (1990). The fifth discipline. New York: Doubleday.

Shaw, R.B. (1997). Trust in the balance: Building successful organizations on results, integrity, and concern. San Francisco: Jossey-Bass.

Schultz, R. (1966). How to handle grievances. Supervision, 28, 10–12.

Sigband, N. B. (1969). Needed: Corporate policies on communications. Advanced Management Journal, 34, 61–67.

Sigband, N. B. (1974). What's happened to employee commitment? Personnel Journal, 53, 131–135.

Stacey, R. D. (1996). Complexity and creativity in organizations. San Francisco: Berrett-Koehler.

Stewart, L. P. (1980). Whistle blowing: Implications for organizational communication. Journal of Communication, 30, 90–101.

Stanton, E.S. (1982). <u>Reality-centered people management: Key to improved productivity</u>. New York: AMACOM.

Steers, R. M. & Porter, L. W. (1983). <u>Motivation and work behavior</u>. New York: McGraw-Hill.

Stevenin, T. J. (1996). <u>People power: Tapping the spirit of quality performance and service in your organization</u>. (publisher undetermined).

Stone, F. (1997). Who would have thought you were capable of this? <u>Getting Results—for the Hands on Manager, 42</u>, 1.

Straub, J. T. (1996). Productive gripe sessions. <u>Getting Results—for the Hands on Manager, 41</u>, 8.

Symon, G. & Cassell (1998). <u>Qualitative methods and analysis in organizational research</u>. Thousand Oaks, CA: Sage.

Sypher, B. D. (Ed.). (1986). <u>Case studies in organizational communication 2: Perspectives on contemporary work life</u>. New York: Guilford.

Taylor, L. K. (1972). <u>Not for bread alone: An appreciation of job enrichment</u>. London: Business Books Limited.

Thompson, V. A. (1976). <u>Bureaucracy and the modern world</u>. Morristown, NJ: General Learning Press.

Timbers, E. (1966). Strengthening motivation through communication. <u>Advanced Management Journal, 31 (April)</u>, 64–69

Toffler, A. (1990). <u>Power shift: Knowledge, wealth, and violence at the edge of the twenty-first century</u>. New York: Bantam.

Tubbs, S. & Widgery, R. N. (1978). When productivity lags, are key managers really communicating? Management Review, 67, 20–25.

Turner, S. P. (1983). Complex organizations as savage tribes. Journal for the Theory of Social Behavior, 7, 99–125.

Vogel, A. (1967). Why don't employees speak up? Personnel Administration, 30, 18–24.

Voich, D. Jr., et al. (1975). Information systems for operations and management. Cincinnati, OH: South-Western.

Wager, L. W. (1972). Organizational linking pins: Hierarchy status and communicative roles in interlevel conferences. Human Relations, 25, 307–326.

Walker, M. B. & Trimboli, A. (1989). Communicating affect: The role of verbal and nonverbal content. Journal of Language and Social Psychology, 8, 229–248.

Walters, K. D. (1975). Your employees' right to blow the whistle. Harvard Business Review, 53, 26–34, 161–162.

Walton, E. (1961). How effective is the grapevine? Personnel Journal, 38, 45–49.

Weber, M. (1966). The theory of social and economic organization. (A. Henderson & T. Parsons, Trans.). New York: Free Press.

Webster, H. (1973). Taboo: A sociological study. New York: Octagon Books.

Weick, K. E. (1969). The social psychology of organizing. Reading, MA: Addison-Wesley.

Woronoff, J. (1983). Japan's wasted workers. Totowa, NJ: Allanheld, Osmun & Co..

APPENDICES

APPENDIX A

SURVEY INSTRUMENT
(ORIGINALLY ADMINISTERED ONLINE)

<u>SURVEY OF ORGANIZATIONAL COMMUNICATION</u>[1]

**Thank you for giving about 10 minutes to fill out this survey.
Your views are very important in the study of
Organizational Communication as well as communication at
your institution.**

Instructions: This survey investigates a phenomenon in organizational communication and how this phenomenon impacts organizational health. In this phenomenon people express their opinions and knowledge about their organization informally (for example, with colleagues, friends, and family), but they do not (have opportunities to) do so formally (for example, with their bosses or at public meetings). As a result, much information concerning the organization that is known in the informal context may remain absent in the formal context. As a further result, such information may not be incorporated in the formulation of organizational policies and plans. For the ease of wording, let's tentatively label this phenomenon "public secrets," that is, public knowledge in one context is secret in another context.

This study has obtained human subjects approval (A copy of the approval form is available at request). The informed consent form is available by clicking <u>here</u>. Your responses are sent to the researcher through the Geocities WebMonitor which completely <u>blocks your e-mail address or dentification</u> (You can view a sample response by click-

---

1.   To protect the identity of the original subject organization, the name of this
      organization has been deleted from the survey instrument.

ing <u>here</u>). <u>Please do not indicate your name</u> in your responses. THANKS!

Section 1: The practice of "public secrets"

1. Do you express and exchange frank opinions (what is intended in conscious privacy) about your institution with colleagues, friends, and/or family, but not with administrators?
    ❑ yes ❑ no ❑ sometimes ❑ do not know

2. Do you express and exchange frank opinions about your institution privately, but not publicly (e.g., at meetings)?
    ❑ yes ❑ no ❑ sometimes ❑ do not know

3. How often do you express frank opinions about your institution informally, but not formally?
    ❑ always ❑ more than twice a day
    ❑ more than twice a week ❑ more than twice a month
    ❑ occasionally ❑ never

4. With whom do you express your frank opinions about your institution? (Please also make an indication of frequency under all applicable groups of people.)
    a. With family
    ❑ always ❑ more than twice a day
    ❑ more than twice a week ❑ more than twice a month
    ❑ occasionally ❑ never
    b. With friends
    ❑ always ❑ more than twice a day
    ❑ more than twice a week ❑ more than twice a month
    ❑ occasionally ❑ never

c. With colleagues

❏ always   ❏ more than twice a day
❏ more than twice a week   ❏ more than twice a month
❏ occasionally   ❏ never

d. With low level administrators (associate dean and lower)

❏ always   ❏ more than twice a day
❏ more than twice a week   ❏ more than twice a month
❏ occasionally   ❏ never

e. With high level administrators (dean and higher)

❏ always   ❏ more than twice a day
❏ more than twice a week   ❏ more than twice a month
❏ occasionally   ❏ never

5. With whom do you **AVOID** expressing frank opinions about your
    institution? (Please also make an indication of frequency under all
    applicable groups of people. **"AVOID"** here includes, when an
    idea comes up in your mind: (a) you intentionally refrain from
    expressing it; (b) you lack an opportunity to express it to the tar-
    geted audience; and (c) you feel too nonchalant to express it
    because you believe such expression results in nothing.)

a. Avoid family

❏ always   ❏ more than twice a day
❏ more than twice a week   ❏ more than twice a month
❏ occasionally   ❏ never

b. Avoid friends

❏ always   ❏ more than twice a day
❏ more than twice a week   ❏ more than twice a month
❏ occasionally   ❏ never

c. Avoid colleagues

❏ always   ❏ more than twice a day
❏ more than twice a week   ❏ more than twice a month
❏ occasionally   ❏ never

d. Avoid low level administrators (associate dean and lower)
❏ always   ❏ more than twice a day
❏ more than twice a week   ❏ more than twice a month
❏ occasionally   ❏ never
e. Avoid high level administrators (dean and higher)
❏ always   ❏ more than twice a day
❏ more than twice a week   ❏ more than twice a month
❏ occasionally   ❏ never

Other comments on this section if above questions and scale of choices do not accommodate your case well:

Section 2: Causes of "public secrets" (People may express views more freely in one context than in another for a variety of reasons. How important do you think each of the following reasons is in influencing YOUR expression of views? Please respond to all those "causes" that you believe are applicable.)

6. a. Fear of losing your job
    ❏ not important ❏ somewhat important ❏ important ❏ very important
    b. Fear of penalty from administration
    ❏ not important ❏ somewhat important ❏ important ❏ very important
    c. Suggestions not acknowledged with actions
    ❏ not important ❏ somewhat important ❏ important ❏ very important
    d. The culture of secrecy
    ❏ not important ❏ somewhat important ❏ important ❏ very important
    e. Hierarchy and/or social stratification
    ❏ not important ❏ somewhat important ❏ important ❏ very important

f. Social desirability

❑ not important ❑ somewhat important ❑ important ❑ very important

g. Lack of opportunities to interact, personally or otherwise, with people to whom you wish to express your ideas

❑ not important ❑ somewhat important ❑ important ❑ very important

Other comments on this section if above questions and scale of choices do not accommodate your case well:

Section 3: Consequences of an organizational culture that contains a high level of "public secrets" (Restraints on free expression may vary from mere discretion to an atmosphere of terror—potentially resulting in severe problems for the organization. Consider each of the possible negative consequences below and indicate degree of severity of all applicable causes?)

7. a. Negative feelings on your part about your institution

❑ not important ❑ somewhat important ❑ important ❑ very important

b. Low morale on your part to contribute extra efforts for your institution

❑ not important ❑ somewhat important ❑ important ❑ very important

c. Negative impact on your quality of work

❑ not important ❑ somewhat important ❑ important ❑ very important

d. Bad communication climate at your institution

❑ not important ❑ somewhat important ❑ important ❑ very important

e. Consideration of locating a new job somewhere else

❑ not important ❑ somewhat important ❑ important ❑ very important

Other comments on this section if above questions and scale of choices do not accommodate your case well:

[text input box]

Section 4: Topics you AVOID discussing formally (with administrators or at public meetings). (Please indicate how often you **avoid** discussion of all those applicable topics. Definition of "avoid" mentioned in Question 5 also applies here.)

8. a. Administration practices
- ❑ always
- ❑ more than twice a day
- ❑ more than twice a week
- ❑ more than twice a month
- ❑ occasionally
- ❑ neverr

b. Problems at your institution
- ❑ always
- ❑ more than twice a day
- ❑ more than twice a week
- ❑ more than twice a month
- ❑ occasionally
- ❑ neverr

c. Suggestions for improvement of your institution
- ❑ always
- ❑ more than twice a day
- ❑ more than twice a week
- ❑ more than twice a month
- ❑ occasionally
- ❑ neverr

d. Colleague performance
- ❑ always
- ❑ more than twice a day
- ❑ more than twice a week
- ❑ more than twice a month
- ❑ occasionally
- ❑ neverr

e. Compensation and benefits
- ❑ always
- ❑ more than twice a day
- ❑ more than twice a week
- ❑ more than twice a month
- ❑ occasionally
- ❑ neverr

f. Well-accepted assumptions that do not work toward the health of
your institution

❑ always   ❑ more than twice a day
❑ more than twice a week   ❑ more than twice a month
❑ occasionally   ❑ neverrr

Other comments on this section if above questions and scale of choices
do not accommodate your case well:

```
┌────────────────────────────────────────┬─┐
│                                        │▲│
│                                        │ │
│                                        │ │
│                                        │ │
│                                        │▼│
├─┬────────────────────────────────────┬─┼─┤
│◄│                                    │►│ │
└─┴────────────────────────────────────┴─┴─┘
```

Section 5: Strategies to increase free expression (Assuming that a
more free expression of views is valuable in promoting organizational
health, consider each of the following strategies and indicate the degree
to which each strategy would be effective in promoting free expression
of views.)

9. a. Suggestion box
    ❑ not important ❑ somewhat important ❑ important ❑ very important
    b. Reward of active voices
    ❑ not important ❑ somewhat important ❑ important ❑ very important
    c. Free-discussion channels through computer network
    ❑ not important ❑ somewhat important ❑ important ❑ very important
    d. Discussion of the "undiscussables" initiated by administration
    ❑ not important ❑ somewhat important ❑ important ❑ very important
    e. Joint meeting participated by both faculty and administration
    ❑ not important ❑ somewhat important ❑ important ❑ very important
    f. Acknowledgement of suggestions with actions as well as with
    words
    ❑ not important ❑ somewhat important ❑ important ❑ very important

Other comments on this section if above questions and scale of choices do not accommodate your case well:

Section 6: Please inform me a bit about yourself.

10. Sex:
    - ❑ Male
    - ❑ Female
11. Total years of your work experience at your institution (including experience as a TA):

    [   ] years
12. Your race/ethnicity (optional):

    [   ]
13. Your annual salary range (optional):
    - ❑ under $40,000
    - ❑ $40,000–$60,000
    - ❑ over $60,000
14. Are you tenured or untenured?
    - ❑ tenured
    - ❑ untenured
15. Your academic rank?
    - ❑ Lecturer
    - ❑ Assistant professor
    - ❑ Associate professor
    - ❑ Professor
16. Your academic unit?
    - ❑ College of Agriculture
    - ❑ College of Applied Sciences and Arts

- ❏ College of Business and Administration
- ❏ College of Education
- ❏ College of Engineering
- ❏ College of Liberal Arts
- ❏ College of Mass Communication and Media Arts
- ❏ College of Science
- ❏ School of Law
- ❏ School of Medicine

Final comments:

☺ **THANK YOU VERY MUCH!**

APPENDIX B

SURVEY ADMINISTRATION SUMMARY

	number of e-mails available	1st selection 42.7%	2nd selection 10.67%	total selected	total responses[*]	response rate
College of Agriculture	46	20	5	25	18	73.3%
College of Applied Sciences and Arts	62	26	7	33	25	75.6%
College of Business Administration	35	15	4	19	13	69.6%
College of Education	154	66	16	82	62	75.4%
College of Engineering	59	25	6	31	14	44.5%
College of Liberal Arts	226	97	24	121	88	73.0%
College of Mass Comm & Media Arts	57	24	6	30	13	42.7%
College of Science	104	44	11	56	27	48.6%
School of Law	36	15	4	19	13	67.7%
School of Medicine	158	67	17	84	35	41.5%
Total	937	400	100	500	308	61.6%

[*]   Unusable responses not included.

APPENDIX C

EXPLANATIONS OF SURVEY CODES

Codes are listed alphabetically:

A-Colleague: avoid colleagues in expressing frank opinions about your institution.

AdmPractice: "administration practices" as a topic avoided in formal discussion.

A-Family: avoid family in expressing frank opinions about your institution.

A-Friends: avoid friends in expressing frank opinions about your institution.

A-HiAdm: avoid high level administrators (dean & higher) in frank expressions about your institution.

A-LoAdm: avoid low level administrators (associate dean & under) in frank expressions about your institution.

Assumptions: "well-accepted assumptions that do not work toward the health of your institution" as a topic avoided in formal discussion.

BadComm: "bad communication climate" as a possible consequence from public secrets.

BadFeel: "negative feelings about your institution" as a possible consequence from public secrets.

Benefits: "compensation & benefits" as a topic avoided in formal discussion.

CMCMA: College of Mass Communication and Media Arts.

CofAg: College of Agriculture.

CofASA: College of Applied Sciences and Arts.

CofBA: College of Business and Administration.

CofEdu: College of Education.

CofEng: College of Engineering.

CofSci: College of Science.

COLA: College of Liberal Arts.

ColegPerform: "colleague performance" as a topic avoided in formal discussion.

CompChannel: "free discussion channels on computer network" as strategy to alleviate public secrets.

D-Undiscussable: "discussion of the 'undiscussables' initiated by administration" as strategy to alleviate public secrets.

F-Personal: frank with family, friends, & colleagues, but not with administrators.

F-Colleague: frank with colleagues.

FearJob: fear of losing job as a possible cause of public secrets.

FearPenalty: fear of penalty from administration as a possible cause of public secrets.

F-Family: frank with family.

F-Frequency: how often are you frank about your institution informally, but not formally.

F-Friends: frank with friends.

F-HiAdm: frank with high administrators (dean & higher).

F-LoAdm: frank with low administrators (associate dean & under).

F-Private: frank privately/informally but not publicly/formally.

Hierarchy: "hierarchy and/or social stratification" as a possible cause of public secrets.

JobChange: "contemplation of job change" as a possible consequence from public secrets.

JointMeet: "joint meeting participated by both faculty and administration" as a strategy to alleviate public secrets.

LawSchool: School of Law.

LoMorale: low morale as a possible consequence from public secrets.

MedSchool: School of Medicine.

NoInteract: "lack of interaction opportunities with target audience" as a cause of public secrets.

Problem: "problems at your institution" as a topic avoided in formal discussion.

Race: race

Rank: academic rank.

RewardVoice: "reward active voices" as a strategy to alleviate public secrets.

Salary: annual salary range.

Secrecy: "culture of secrecy" as a possible cause of public secrets.

Sex: sex

SocDesire: "social desirability" as a possible cause of public secrets.

Suggest+: "suggestions unacknowledged with actions" as a possible cause of public secrets.

Suggestion: "suggestions for improvement of your institution" as a topic avoided in formal discussion.

SuggestBox: "suggestion box" as strategy to alleviate public secrets.

Tenure: "Are you tenured or untenured?"

Unit: academic unit.

W/Action: "acknowledgement of suggestions with actions" as a strategy to alleviate public secrets.

-WorkQuality: "negative impact on quality of work" as a possible consequence from pulbic secrets.

WkYrs: total years of work experience at your institution (including experience as a TA)

APPENDIX D

INTERVIEW PROTOCOL

"'Public Secrets' as a Phenomenon in Organizational Communication"

Instructions: Please check or fill out all items that apply (you may refuse to answer any of them and all reasonable steps are taken to protect your confidentiality).

I.   Demographic Information

1.   Sex:
   ❏ Male
   ❏ Female
2.   Total years of your work experience at your institution (including experience as a TA): _____ years.
3.   Your race/ethnicity (optional): _____
4.   Your annual salary range (optional):
   ❏ under $40,000
   ❏ $40,000–$60,000
   ❏ over $60,000
5.   Are you tenured or untenured?
   ❏ tenured
   ❏ untenured
6.   Your academic rank?
   ❏ Assistant professor
   ❏ Associate professor
   ❏ Professor
7.   Your academic unit?
   ❏ College of Agriculture
   ❏ College of Applied Sciences and Arts
   ❏ College of Business and Administration
   ❏ College of Education

❑ College of Engineering
❑ College of Liberal Arts
❑ College of Mass Communication and Media Arts
❑ College of Science
❑ School of Law
❑ School of Medicine

II. Questions

1. Do you believe that you genuinely express your feelings, ideas, and knowledge about your institution informally (with family, friends, and colleagues), but not formally (e.g., with administrators or at public meetins)?

2. Do you think your colleagues do this?

3. How often do you think you and your colleagues practice this?

4. What do you think are possible causes that contribute to the emergence of public secrets?

5. What do you think are possible consequences from the phenomenon of public secrets?

6. What topics do you believe you and your colleagues talk about in the informal situation, but not in the formal situation?

7. What tactics or strategies do you know or can you think of that may help alleviate this phenomenon? That is, people may begin to genuinely express and exchange their feelings, ideas, and knowledge about your institution in situations where they did not use to engage in genuine expression?

0-595-27370-X